JILL GORDON'S
CROSS STITCH
PICTURES

JILL GORDON'S
CROSS STITCH
PICTURES

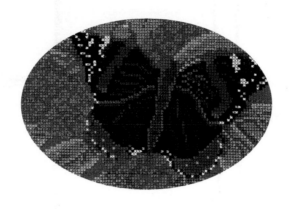

David & Charles

To Holly, Lucy, Peter and Kate,
with love and thanks for your patience
and support through difficult times.

A DAVID & CHARLES BOOK

First published in the UK in 2001

Text and designs Copyright © Jill Gordon 2001
Photography and layout Copyright ©
David & Charles 2001

Jill Gordon has asserted her right to be identified as
author of this work in accordance with the Copyright,
Designs and Patents Act, 1988.

A catalogue record for this book is available
from the British Library.

ISBN 0 7153 0993 5

Book design by Chris and Jane Lanaway
Styled photography by Michelle Garrett
Detail photography by Stuart Batley, Alan Duns
and David Johnson
Printed in Italy by Lego SpA
for David & Charles
Brunel House   Newton Abbot   Devon

Contents

Introduction

Creating the designs for this book has been an exciting and interesting challenge. My previous textile designs have been worked for the most part in wools (yarns) on canvas and my first real venture into cross stitch was a design called March Hares, a picture of two hares in a rolling English landscape. That design became the starting point for this book and the main idea was to try to capture the realism and richness of nature as depicted in my needlepoint designs, but in the different medium of embroidery threads and the coloured fabrics used in cross stitch.

The way I work is very simple. Fortunately, as soon as I start thinking of projects for a book, many ideas spring to mind. This is helped enormously by the beautiful countryside in which I live, and the memories of living in hotter climes, with the profusion of flowers that surrounded me there.

I do small pencil sketches of ideas until they seem to have the right balance, then I work up a larger watercolour sketch that forms the basis of the embroidery design. Sometimes elements are altered as I work and colours are changed. It always surprises me how much the colours alter when they are interpreted in threads. Shades that look wonderful in paintings suddenly look too

heavy when stitched in the more opaque materials of embroidery threads. Once the whole design is stitched, I may alter little details here and there but wherever possible I leave any alterations until the end. This is something I learned from working with Kaffe Fassett: if you alter things as you go along, you may never reach a satisfactory end. Colours that look strange together as you stitch them, often look wonderful when the whole design is complete.

I have used many of my favourite subjects in this book – flowers, wildlife, water and landscapes. I thoroughly enjoyed creating these designs and hope you gain even more pleasure from stitching them.

You should find the book very easy to use.

There are fourteen cross stitch designs, each illustrated with a large colour photograph of the finished project and the projects are accompanied by my own watercolour paintings. The charts are in full colour with symbols and are easy to follow, and all the projects have a list of materials you will need to complete the stitching, followed by detailed guidelines. Anchor stranded cotton (floss) has been used predominantly for the stitching, with one skein per colour used unless otherwise stated.

At the back of the book, on pages 118–125, is information on materials and equipment needed and on useful basic techniques, including how to work all the stitches and how to make up the designs into a variety of delightful items.

The Cottage Garden

This design was inspired partly by wishful thinking when looking at my rather neglected garden and partly by the many beautiful gardens in neighbouring villages; childhood memories have also contributed to its creation. In most of the places that I have lived, we have had large, copiously flowering buddleias, and I can remember vividly the vast numbers of peacock and red admiral butterflies that used to feed on these plants.

RIGHT *The cottage garden, shown here as a pillow but which is equally suitable for a framed picture, is a rich reminder of country cottage gardens. The red admiral or peacock butterfly would also make a lovely motif repeated to edge a pillow or tea towel.*

Butterflies are like one's memories of summer – just as summers seemed to be much longer and hotter when I was a child, there also seemed to be more butterflies. This may well be true, as modern farming methods seem to have decimated much of our wildlife. Luckily, in the part of England that is now my home, very little spraying goes on, so there are masses of nettles and thistles for the caterpillars to feed on. Although these plants are considered unsightly and a sign of neglect, they are great favourites with butterfly larvae: thistles are particularly liked by peacock larvae and nettles are the staple food of the red admiral larvae. Adult peacocks and red admirals can regularly be seen sunning themselves on buddleia, just as they are in my design – which is why I have planted two types in my garden.

When it came to choosing flowers for the cottage garden, hollyhocks and delphiniums were a natural choice as both are great favourites of mine. In Croatia, where I lived for some years, hollyhocks grew wild in many wonderful colours in great abundance. They are also a traditional cottage garden flower, as are the delphiniums, which provide a brilliant splash of blue in the garden and lead the eye to the beds of lavender.

Finding the right cottage to work from provided just the excuse I needed to travel around neighbouring villages. I am wonderfully positioned on the edge of the Peak District National Park to see a variety of traditional cottages. I made sketches of many different houses and gardens, taking photographs and making sketches before coming up with my final design. The cottage here is a typical, well-to-do, Derbyshire thatched cottage with roses covering the front. These flowers are another favourite of mine, especially the rambling fragrant varieties such as the wonderfully perfumed Albertine rose. Its lovely peachy coloured blooms can still be found adorning many country houses. Here it is interspersed with purple clematis to give some variety of colour.

As many of my previous designs have been for needlepoint where the entire canvas is stitched, I found it an enjoyable challenge stitching this garden and being able to leave parts of the background fabric bare, which then became an active part of the design by suggesting foliage or shadow. It is also fascinating for me to see how differently light reflects from embroidery threads instead of wools (yarns), and the resulting texture from cross stitch rather than needlepoint stitches.

PLAN OF CHARTS

1	2	3
4	5	6

CHART 1

KEY

Anchor stranded cotton (floss)

2	72	131	242	255	371	904	
13	98	140	244 (2 skeins)	256	382	905	
49	99	142	246	257	403	945	
60	118	175	253	295	888 (2 skeins)	1004	
68	119	212	254	326	898	1028	

CHART 2

KEY

Anchor stranded cotton (floss)

⠒	2	■	72	◢	131	✛	242	✖	255	◣	371	◥	904
I	13	C	98	≡	140	▼	244 (2 skeins)	Z	256	◪	382	■	905
W	49	▶	99	▬	142	◐	246	✳	257	▬	403	✦	945
人	60	O	118	∩	175	✗	253	M	295	╱	888 (2 skeins)	⏚	1004
⠿	68	◀	119	◣	212	◣	254	V	326	◣	898	◢	1028

CHART 3

CHART 4

KEY

Anchor stranded cotton (floss)

	2		72		131		242		255		371		904
	13		98		140		244 (2 skeins)		256		382		905
	49		99		142		246		257		403		945
	60		118		175		253		295		888 (2 skeins)		1004
	68		119		212		254		326		898		1028

CHART 5

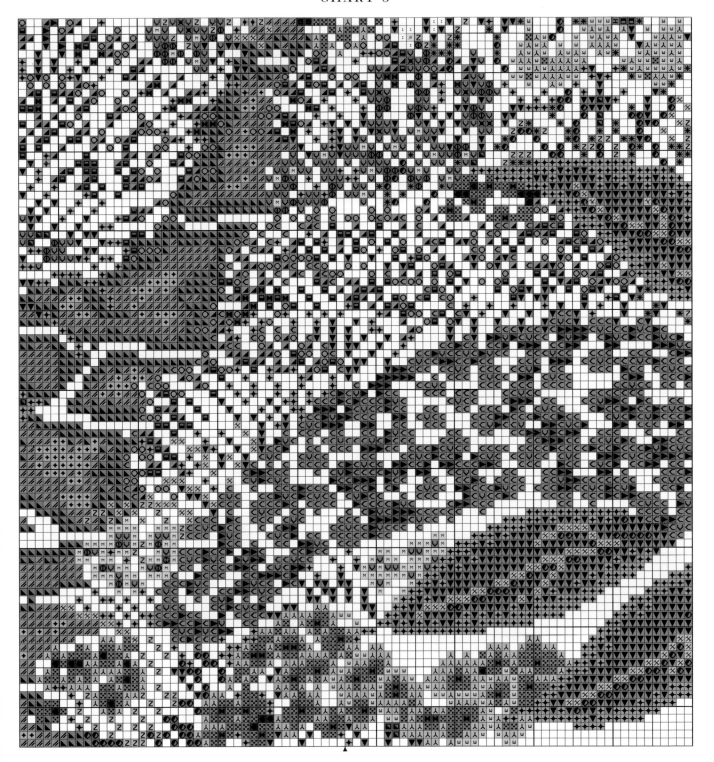

CHART 6

KEY

Anchor stranded cotton (floss)

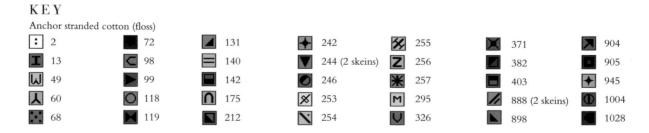

⸪ 2	■ 72	◩ 131	✦ 242	✗ 255	◆ 371	◥ 904
I 13	◀ 98	═ 140	▼ 244 (2 skeins)	Z 256	◢ 382	▣ 905
W 49	▶ 99	▣ 142	◐ 246	✳ 257	▭ 403	✦ 945
⅄ 60	○ 118	∩ 175	✗ 253	M 295	�ि 888 (2 skeins)	Φ 1004
⸬ 68	◄ 119	◣ 212	◸ 254	∪ 326	◣ 898	■ 1028

THE COTTAGE GARDEN

DESIGN SIZE

18in x 13¼in (46cm x 34cm) approximately

Stitch count: 252 x 185

MATERIALS

- 24in x 20in (61cm x 51cm) 14-count Aida
  in teal green (Zweigart No.626)
- Size 24 or 26 tapestry needle
- Anchor stranded cottons (floss) as listed in the key

STITCHING GUIDELINES

I suggest that you begin stitching at the centre with this design as the whole of the fabric is not solidly stitched. Begin by finding and marking the centre of your fabric (see Techniques, page 119). Stitching will be quicker and easier if you arrange your thread colours on an organiser before you begin (see Techniques, page 119).

The whole design is worked in full cross stitches using two threads of stranded cotton (floss) throughout. Beginning with Anchor 60 (light pink) carefully stitch that colour in. Have another needle threaded with two threads of Anchor 68 (medium pink) to fill in around the first colour. From this area, you can move out to either side to stitch the largest elements, the hollyhocks and delphiniums, moving down to the butterflies and the buddleia.

When all the stitching is complete, remove the tacking (basting) guidelines or markings and use a steam iron to gently press on the wrong side of the work.

Make your work up into a cushion following the instructions in Making Up, page 123 or, if you prefer, frame it as a picture, following the instructions on page 125.

The Peacock

Peacocks are such wonderfully iridescent, almost mythical birds. I have marvelled at their beauty and been entranced by the shimmering display of that glorious metallic bronze and blue-green tail with its dancing eyes. The idea of stitching a peacock as a circular design – echoing the actual shape of a peacock's raised tail – with feathers fanning out over the whole area, has been in my mind for many years, and this seemed a perfect opportunity to bring it into being.

RIGHT *I have used this design to make an eye-catching footstool but it could be used in other ways. For example, it would look quite beautiful set under glass as a table-top or made into a wonderfully plump, circular cushion.*

Throughout my life, I have experienced the beauty of peacocks at close quarters: at Drusillas, near Eastbourne (one of Britain's earliest nature parks) when I was a child; in the park at Cheltenham when I was studying; and most recently at a nearby farm. Here, the peacocks wander around with the chickens and perch on the barn roofs in the evening, giving almighty screeches at the walkers passing by: I can certainly see why on many a country estate, as well as providing splendid colour with their gleaming, rainbow-like elegance, peacocks have been used as 'guard dogs'. Occasionally I have seen them floating down from their treetop roosts. What an amazing and exotic sight that is, and for a short space of time I am transported to warmer, sunnier climes.

Peacocks in art and design have interested me a great deal and they have certainly influenced this design in many ways. I have looked at the way in which Japanese painters have depicted peacocks, in fine detail, using a combination of stylisation and realism and I have reached for that effect. This is also a genre much used by Kaffe Fassett with whom I studied and worked for many years.

The peacock in my design possesses a many-eyed tail. The more eyes the peacock has on his tail, the more attractive he is to peafowl as the eyes are presumed to show his strength and fitness. Unfortunately, an extravagantly opulent tail, however attractive, is a major disadvantage in another way. It is so cumbersome it makes flight difficult and therefore makes it easier for the peacock to fall prey to predators, and further decreases his chances of survival.

The peacock's 'eyes' certainly make him attractive to stitch and the shape lends itself admirably to the circular footstool.

I have used some Kreinik metallic threads – a Very Fine (#4) Braid – and some shiny Anchor Marlitt rayon to suggest the iridescent quality of the feathers. There are many changes of colours and hues, suggesting the shimmering quality of the peacock.

A border of peacock feather 'eyes' completes the design perfectly and provides a natural boundary to the sumptuous tail. I have used a navy blue Aida fabric to suggest fullness without having to stitch every part of the material. When working on a dark fabric, it always helps to place some white material or paper underneath the work so that you can see the holes in the fabric when you are stitching.

PLAN OF CHARTS

1	2	3
4	5	6

CHART 1

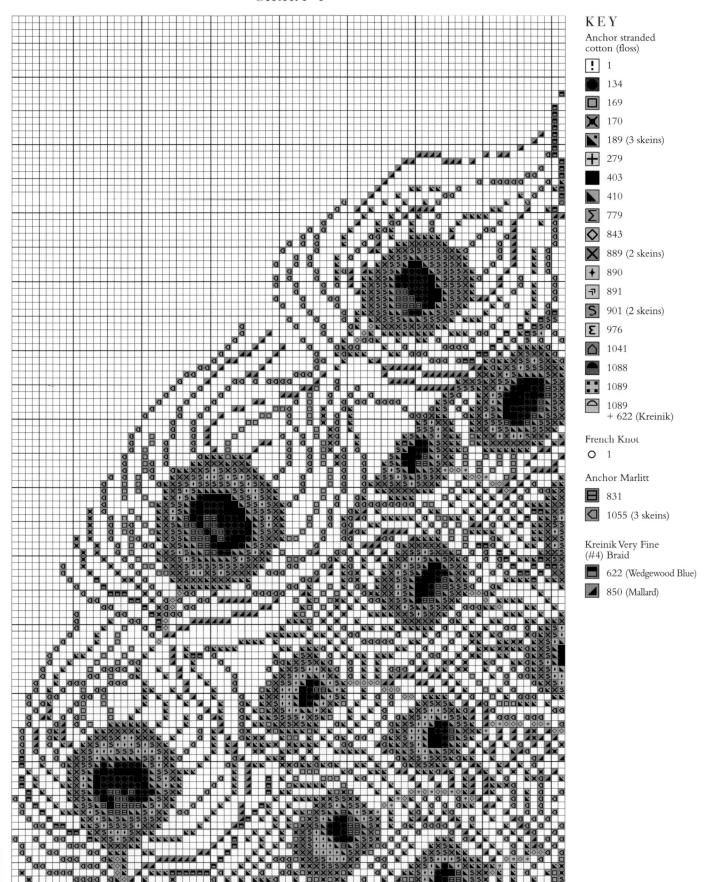

KEY

Anchor stranded
cotton (floss)

!	1
■	134
□	169
✕	170
◩	189 (3 skeins)
✚	279
■	403
◣	410
Σ	779
◇	843
✕	889 (2 skeins)
✦	890
ꓶ	891
S	901 (2 skeins)
ℇ	976
⌂	1041
◪	1088
⣏	1089
⌂	1089 + 622 (Kreinik)

French Knot

| ○ | 1 |

Anchor Marlitt

| ⊟ | 831 |
| ◁ | 1055 (3 skeins) |

Kreinik Very Fine
(#4) Braid

| ⬛ | 622 (Wedgewood Blue) |
| ◣ | 850 (Mallard) |

CHART 2

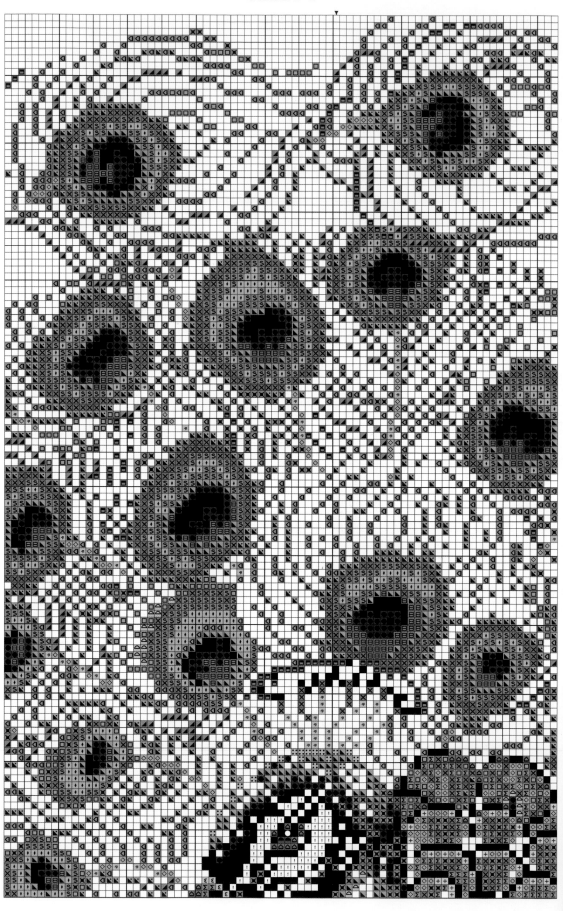

KEY

Anchor stranded cotton (floss)

⊡	1
●	134
▢	169
✕	170
◣	189 (3 skeins)
✚	279
■	403
◥	410
Σ	779
◇	843
✕	889 (2 skeins)
✦	890
⊐	891
S	901 (2 skeins)
Ɛ	976
⌂	1041
⬬	1088
⊡	1089
⌓	1089 + 622 (Kreinik)

French Knot

○	1

Anchor Marlitt

▥	831
◁	1055 (3 skeins)

Kreinik Very Fine (#4) Braid

◨	622 (Wedgewood Blue)
◣	850 (Mallard)

CHART 3

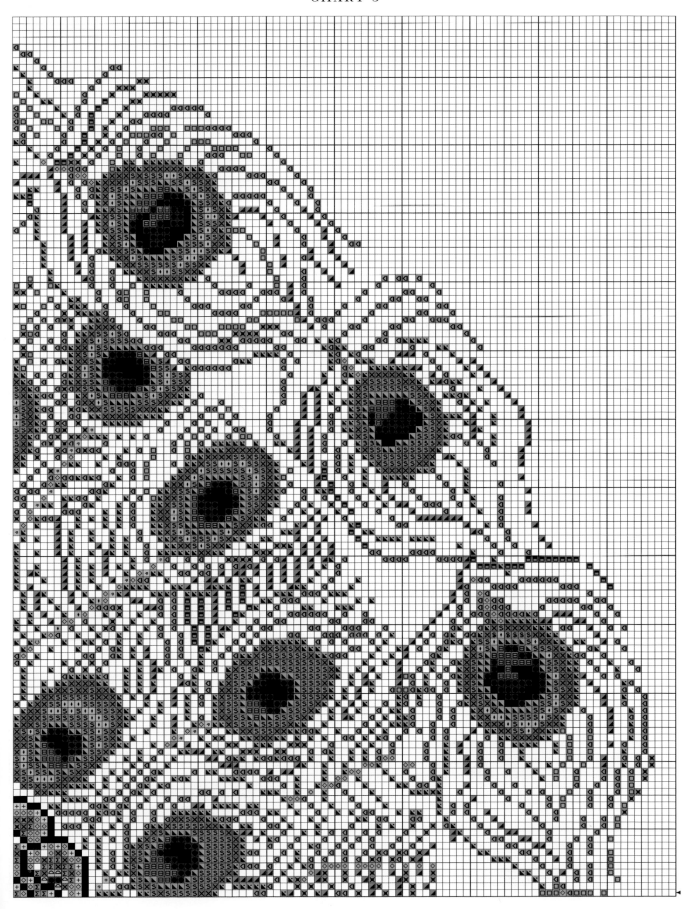

CHART 4

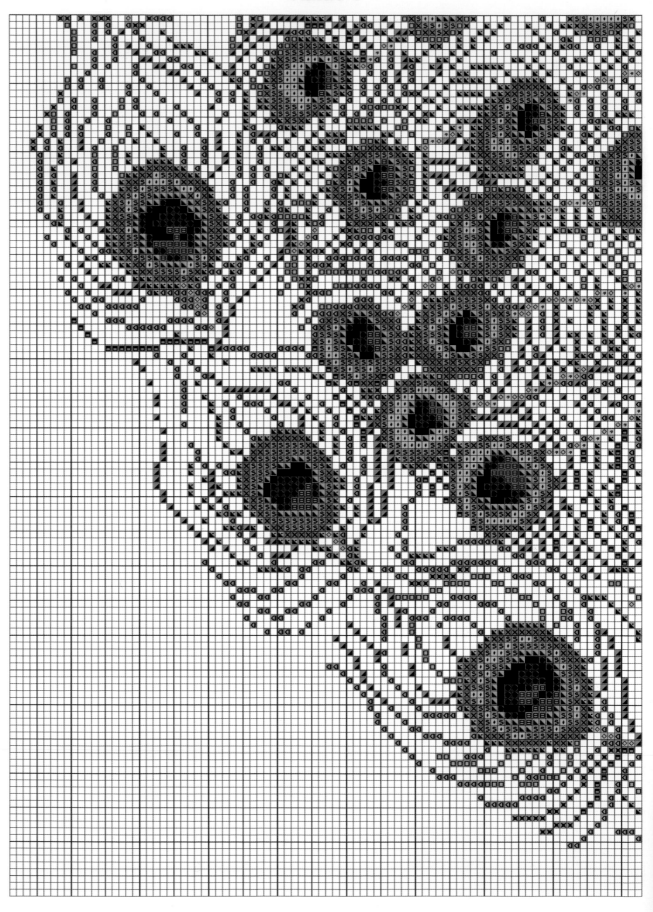

CHART 5

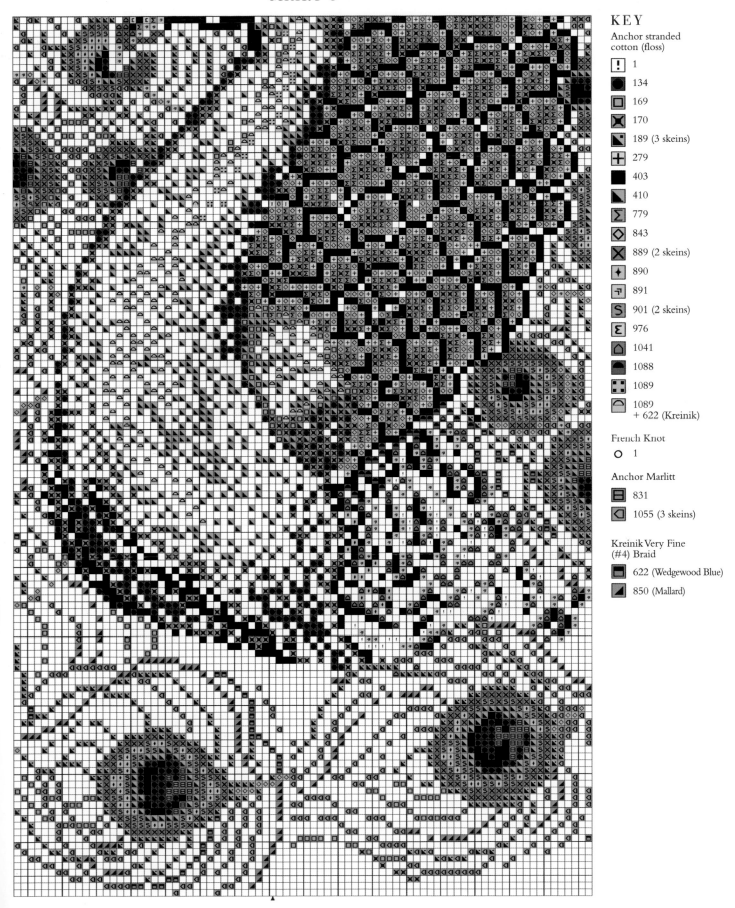

KEY

Anchor stranded cotton (floss)

☒	1
●	134
☐	169
☒	170
◼	189 (3 skeins)
✚	279
■	403
◣	410
Σ	779
◇	843
☒	889 (2 skeins)
✦	890
⊣	891
S	901 (2 skeins)
Σ	976
⌂	1041
◓	1088
⠿	1089
⌂	1089 + 622 (Kreinik)

French Knot

○	1

Anchor Marlitt

⊟	831
◁	1055 (3 skeins)

Kreinik Very Fine (#4) Braid

▬	622 (Wedgewood Blue)
◤	850 (Mallard)

CHART 6

KEY

Anchor stranded cotton (floss)

!	1
●	134
◻	169
⊠	170
◣	189 (3 skeins)
✛	279
■	403
◥	410
Σ	779
◇	843
✕	889 (2 skeins)
✦	890
⅂	891
S	901 (2 skeins)
Ɛ	976
⌂	1041
⬤	1088
▦	1089
⬠	1089 + 622 (Kreinik)

French Knot

○	1

Anchor Marlitt

⊟	831
◁	1055 (3 skeins)

Kreinik Very Fine (#4) Braid

▤	622 (Wedgewood Blue)
◢	850 (Mallard)

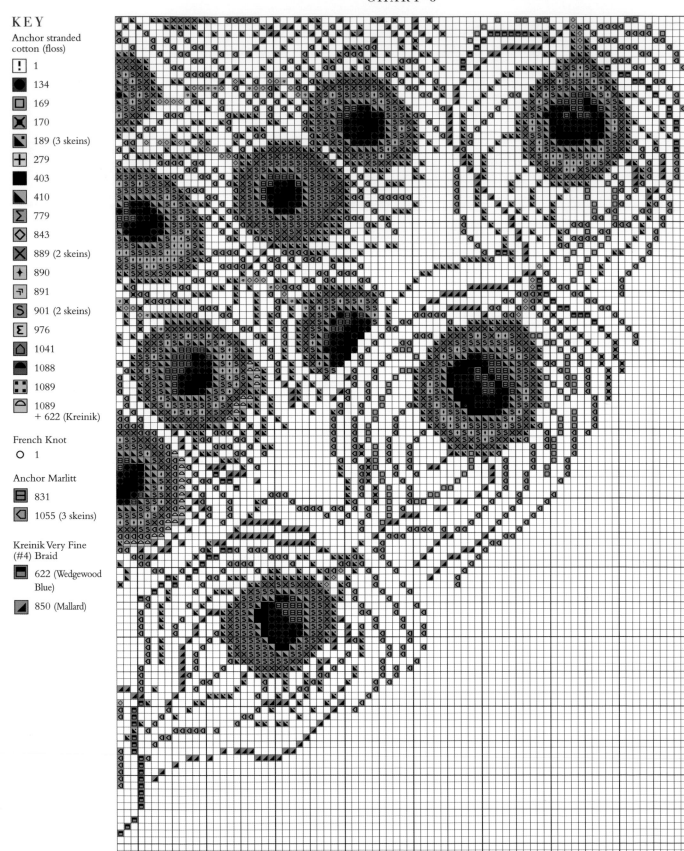

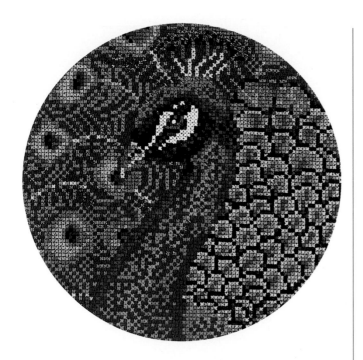

THE PEACOCK

DESIGN SIZE
18½in (47cm) diameter approximately
Stitch count: 259 diameter

MATERIALS

♦ 26in x 26in (66cm x 66cm) 14-count Aida in navy
blue (Coats No.589)

♦ Size 26 or 24 tapestry needle

♦ Anchor stranded cottons (floss) and Anchor Marlitt
as listed in the key

♦ Kreinik Very Fine (#4) Braids: 622 (Wedgewood
blue) and 850 (Mallard)

STITCHING GUIDELINES

Begin by finding and marking the centre of your
fabric (see Techniques, page 119). You will also find
stitching easier if you sort out your threads on an
organiser (see page 119).

Two threads of stranded cotton (floss) are used to
work the cross stitches unless otherwise marked on the
chart. When mixing stranded cotton (floss) with

Kreinik Very Fine (#4) Braid 622, use one thread of
each. Anchor Marlitt comes in four-stranded skeins
and two strands should be used in this design.

Begin at the centre of the design, using two threads
of stranded cotton (floss) 170 (dark kingfisher), and
work towards the peacock's eye. Then work 1 (white),
403 (black), 134 (blue) and the other colours shown
on the chart that form the peacock's head.

Once the head is completed it will give you a
central focus to work from. Stitch the face and crown,
being careful to count accurately to ensure the right
positioning, then bring the peacock to life by working
one French knot in white to highlight the eye (see
Techniques, page 121).

Now work down the peacock's neck and breast,
moving on to the small fan-like feathers to the right of
his neck. This is the most intense area of stitching and
once this is completed, you will find it much easier to
move on outwards, working the eyes and feathers.

Leave the border until last, as, if you have
miscounted in any way, it will be easier to add or
subtract stitches before the border is stitched. This is
such a large, airy design, that as long as the peacock's
face, neck and breast are accurate, a miscounted stitch
here or there will not be crucial.

When all the stitching is complete, remove the
tacking (basting) guidelines or markings. Steam iron
the work carefully on the
wrong side taking care
not to press too hard as
this flattens the stitches
and spoils the texture of
the embroidery.
Instructions for making
the finished design into a
footstool cover are in
Making Up on page 124.

The Summer Orchard

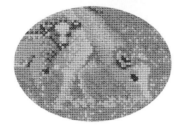

It has always been a personal idyll: the

tranquil beauty of an early summer orchard

with the comfortable sound of cows lazily

tearing at mouthfuls of grass.

I am fortunate enough to live in delightful

countryside on the edge of the Peak District

in England, where I can step out of my

cottage door and see just such a scene. Most

of the non-milking cows are the same lovely

warm mushroom colour as the ones I have

depicted in this design.

RIGHT *In the late spring and early summer in England,
wild cherry, pear, apple and hawthorn blossoms abound and
at that time the cows in the farm orchards appear just as
these in this picture.*

valuable lessons I learned when I was studying and working with Kaffe, was not to be afraid of using inspirations that you see in other people's work. When you take different elements from many different sources to form a design, you bring it together with your own vision and the result is totally your own.

The main blossom tree was a delight to stitch and the whole summery feel of the piece is fun to do in the winter when the short grey days seem to make it a long time to live through before enjoying the sun and the first flowers of spring again.

Often when designing, a number of ideas gleaned from many different sources come together. With this design, although the first inspiration was from watching the cows nearby, other images glimpsed at different times have come into play too. For instance a beautiful painting called Blossom Time, which featured in one of Kaffe Fassett's diaries, and a photograph of cows in an orchard in France, to name but two. One of the most

PLAN OF CHARTS

1	2
3	4

CHART 1

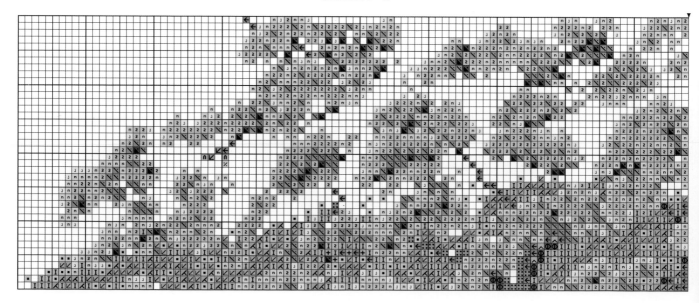

THE SUMMER ORCHARD

DESIGN SIZE

14in x 9⅞in (35.5cm x 25cm) approximately

Stitch count: 196 x 139

MATERIALS

- ◆ 18in x 14in (47cm x 35.5cm) 14-count Aida in light blue (Coats No.4600)
- ◆ Size 24 or 26 tapestry needle
- ◆ Anchor stranded cottons (floss) as listed in the key

STITCHING GUIDELINES

The whole design is worked in full cross stitches using two threads of stranded cotton (floss) throughout.

Begin by finding and marking the centre of your fabric (see Techniques, page 119). You will also find stitching easier and quicker if you sort your threads on an organiser (see page 119).

If you wish to stitch the design from the centre outwards, begin at the centre point on the chart, using two threads of Anchor 888 (light trunk brown). Work outwards moving from this central stitch, changing to the other marked colours when required. You may find it helpful to outline the upper branch of the main trunk by stitching in 277 (medium trunk brown) to give a good guideline.

If you prefer to stitch the design along the bottom upwards, ensure first that the design will have an adequate border of unstitched fabric left all around it. Start at the bottom left-hand corner using two threads

KEY

Anchor stranded cotton (floss)

j 2	⊘ 236	← 277	▫ 368	◺ 874
n 49 (2 skeins)	◿ 238	I 280	⊠ 369	⬓ 888
◥ 68	⟋ 254	⋈ 289	c 387	◤ 890
◼ 69	⋒ 255 (2 skeins)	⧉ 290	✚ 388	2 1094 (2 skeins)
⧅ 227	▪ 261	▼ 358	S 855	
	◺ 267	⊓ 366	N 856	

CHART 2

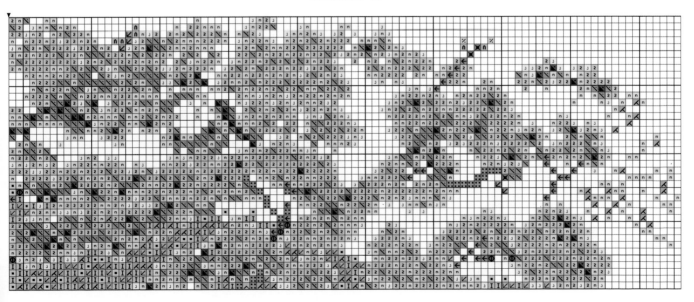

CHART 3

KEY

Anchor stranded
cotton (floss)

j	2		236		277	·	368		874
n	49 (2 skeins)		238	I	280		369		888
	68		254	M	289	c	387		890
	69	n	255 (2 skeins)		290		388	2	1094 (2 skeins)
	227	·	261		358	S	855		
			267		366	N	856		

CHART 4

of 238 (dark green), filling in that area with 255 (medium grass green) and dotting in the 227 (shadow green). Continue in this manner to work your way right across the bottom of the design, working upwards with different colours as and when required.

Regardless of the direction of stitching, I suggest that you stitch the cows, the grass and the main trunk and blossoms before working the trees in the background.

When all the stitching is complete, remove the tacking (basting) guidelines or markings. Gently steam iron the wrong side of the design, ironing out any creases but being careful not to press too hard as this will flatten the stitches.

Frame the picture, choosing a frame and mount board you like and which set off the colours in the design (see Making Up, page 125 for framing).

The Formal Garden

Gardens of all designs are wonderful sources

of inspiration and this project brought

together my love of garden statuary, formal

gardens and water all in one piece! The idea

of the greyhounds came from the garden of

Harold Peto who was an architect with an

Arts and Crafts background. He collected

many garden treasures on his travels in Italy

and these can be seen at Iford Manor in

Wiltshire, England. I loved the elegant lines of

these beautiful dogs set on pedestals.

RIGHT *This Formal Garden design would make a good companion to the Cottage Garden design (see page 8) and the two would look wonderful sitting together on a sofa as elegant cushions or as a pair of pictures.*

master at using few colours to achieve an extremely complicated, multicoloured effect, his maxim to others is always to 'use lots of colours' – and for the most part, I do. Both methods are extremely interesting and I find it a good exercise to limit the number of colours in a design, sometimes, in order to be more imaginative with where the colours can be used. For example, using mauves or blues for shadows instead of assuming that they will be grey or charcoal.

Both the sunken garden and the fountain beyond were inspired by a visit to another beautiful garden, coincidentally also designed by Harold Peto. The formal gardens completing the picture were suggested to me by the stately grandeur of the gardens at Villandry in the Loire Valley, France. Although Villandry is probably best known for its mixture of ornamental fruit and vegetables, it also has clipped box hedges outlining flower beds in complex symbolic designs.

I included topiary in the garden because it is a fascinating art form that has been practised in gardens around the world for more than 2,000 years. The time, patience and skill involved to create these living sculptures make needlepoint and cross stitch seem quite hasty by comparison!

Traditionally, formal gardens, especially knot gardens, use different coloured gravel and pebbles to draw attention to the different aspects of the patterns but I thought that I had probably used quite enough colours by this point! I learned to stitch and design with Kaffe Fassett and although he is an absolute

When I design a piece like this, I usually have a picture in my mind which I do a rough pencil sketch of, then I look at photographs I have taken, go through my books and sometimes go off on a 'field trip' to do more sketches and take more photographs. So I have the image in mind to begin with and then look for sources to actually work from and bring it all together. It is then very satisfying when the garden comes to life in the form of stitches.

PLAN OF CHARTS

1	2	3
4	5	6

CHART 1

KEY

Anchor stranded
cotton (floss)

60	242	258 (2 skeins)	905	1039 (3 skeins)
68	244	280	945 (3 skeins)	1045
212	246	886	1013	5975
216	255	888 (2 skeins)	1014	
240	256	898	1028	
	257 (2 skeins)	904 (2 skeins)	1037	

CHART 2

KEY

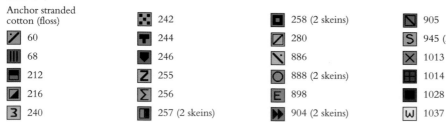

Anchor stranded
cotton (floss)

60	
68	
212	
216	
240	

242	
244	
246	
255	
256	
257 (2 skeins)	

258 (2 skeins)	
280	
886	
888 (2 skeins)	
898	
904 (2 skeins)	

905	
945 (3 skeins)	
1013	
1014	
1028	
1037	

1039 (3 skeins)	
1045	
5975	

CHART 3

CHART 4

KEY

Anchor stranded
cotton (floss)

60	242	258 (2 skeins)	905	1039 (3 skeins)
68	244	280	945 (3 skeins)	1045
212	246	886	1013	5975
216	255	888 (2 skeins)	1014	
240	256	898	1028	
	257 (2 skeins)	904 (2 skeins)	1037	

CHART 5

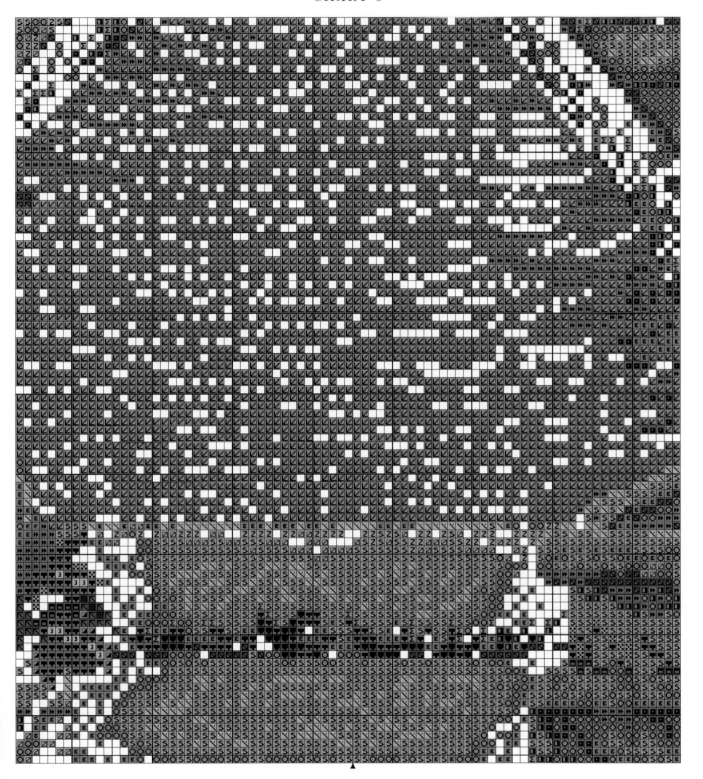

CHART 6

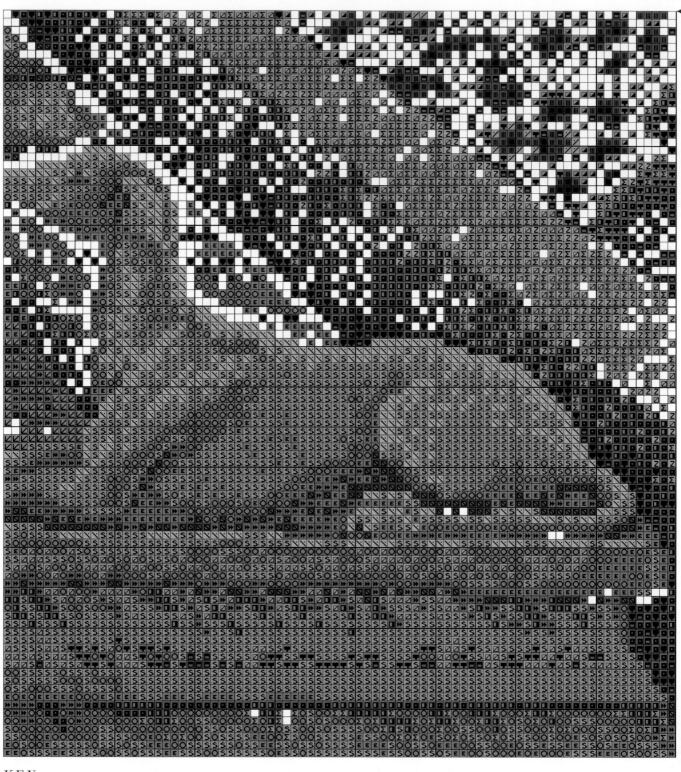

KEY

Anchor stranded
cotton (floss)

 60

242	258 (2 skeins)	905	1039 (3 skeins)
244	280	945 (3 skeins)	1045
246	886	1013	5975
255	888 (2 skeins)	1014	
256	898	1028	
257 (2 skeins)	904 (2 skeins)	1037	

68
212
216
240

THE FORMAL GARDEN

DESIGN SIZE
17¾in x 13¼in (45cm x 34cm) approximately
Stitch count: 250 x 186

MATERIALS
- 24in x 20in (61cm x 51cm) 14-count Aida in teal green (Zweigart No.626)
- Size 24 or 26 tapestry needle
- Anchor stranded cottons (floss) as listed in the key

STITCHING GUIDELINES
The design is worked in whole cross stitches using two strands of stranded cotton (floss) throughout.

Following the guidelines in Techniques, page 119, find and mark the centre of the fabric. I also suggest sorting all your threads in an organiser, which will make stitching easier and quicker.

The design can be stitched from left to right or top to bottom, but try to avoid rubbing on stitching already completed. Alternatively, you may find it easier to work outwards from the centre.

When the stitching is completed, remove any tacking (basting) or guidelines and steam iron it gently on the wrong side, being careful not to press too hard as this tends to flatten the stitches.

Make the stitched design up into a pillow or cushion following the instructions in Making Up, page 123. Alternatively you could frame it as a picture following the instructions on page 125 or make it up into a wall hanging (see page 125).

Nature's Realm

These two wildlife studies, Seals on the Giant's Causeway and Highland Stag, make good partners, displaying beautiful creatures in their natural habitat. A grey seal and her pup rest on the impressive rock formation of the Giant's Causeway in Northern Ireland, while a handsome red stag poses amid Scottish moorland above a loch. Both designs have a Celtic flavour – the seals bordered by an authentic Celtic knot pattern, and the stag framed by a border based on the Nicholson tartan.

RIGHT *These two stunning designs make excellent companions. They were conceived as pictures but would also be perfect for making up into cushions or tray inserts.*

Seals on the Giant's Causeway

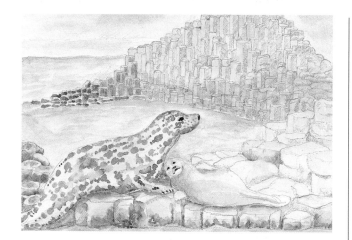

This design features a grey seal with her pup. Almost half of the world population of grey seals occurs around Britain and so, with a bit of luck, it is possible to see them in their natural surroundings. The young are born with creamy white coats, which moult by the time the pups are about four weeks old.

They are also weaned by then and ready for independent life. There are enormous variations in the patterns and colouring of female grey seals and this particular female was a wonderfully spotted one.

As a child I lived on the south coast of England and in north Somerset, and grew up thinking that the sea around Britain was like a not very clear and

PLAN OF CHARTS

1	2
3	4

CHART 1

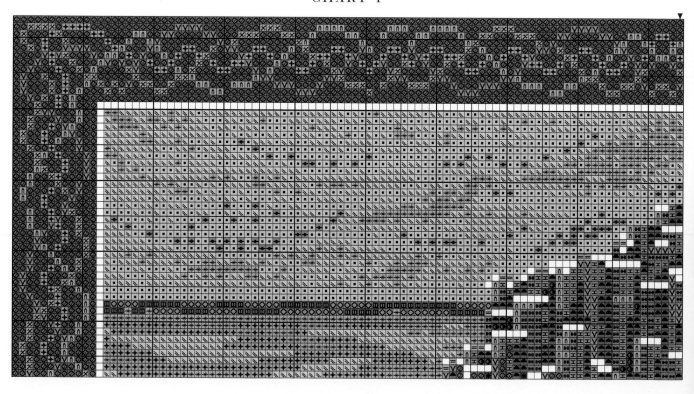

extremely cold soup. So, I was very pleasantly surprised by the wonderfully clear water in Ireland, and since then I have discovered many parts of the British Isles that have lovely coastlines and transparent sea – as on the northern coast of County Antrim, Ireland where the Giant's Causeway is to be found.

What an incredible sight it is too – around 40,000 basalt columns packed tightly together, mostly in the shape of irregular hexagons. It was formed by volcanic eruptions 12 million years ago, the lava cooling and contracting to form these extraordinarily striking shapes. The tops of the columns create stepping stones leading from the foot of the cliff into the sea. The tallest are as high as 40ft (12m) and the solidified lava in the cliffs is as much as 90ft (27m) thick in places.

Our ancestors, however, had different ideas of how it was formed. It was said that Finn McCool, a giant, fell in love with a lady giant who lived on Staffa, an island in the Hebrides, and he built this causeway to bring her across to County Antrim. I believe that there are remnants of a causeway on the west coast of Scotland near Port Patrick. Whatever its origins, the Causeway is an excellent resting place for grey seals and it was quite a challenge stitching the stone columns, making them upright without being too uniform and trying to convey a stone feeling to them.

KEY

Anchor stranded cotton (floss)

✳ 167	▪ 274	✳ 846	⊞ 888	◆ 1040	
Ⅲ 216	✕ 279	Ⅰ 855	⊠ 898	◣ 1041	
═ 264	Σ 280	◠ 856	✦ 926	○ 1064	
◑ 273	V 843	✛ 875	◤ 928	French knot	
	⊘ 845 (3 skeins)	⦂ 885	⋒ 945	○ 926	

CHART 2

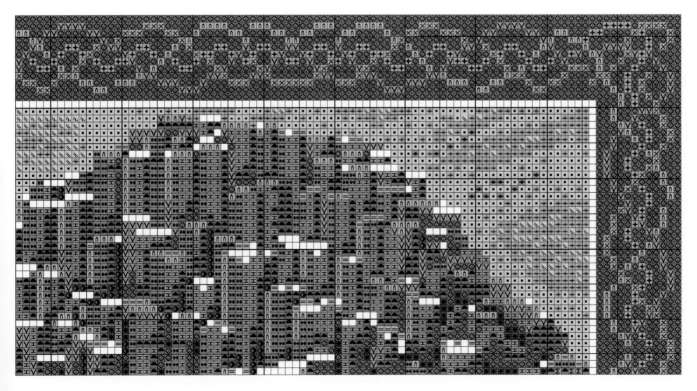

CHART 3

KEY

Anchor stranded
cotton (floss)

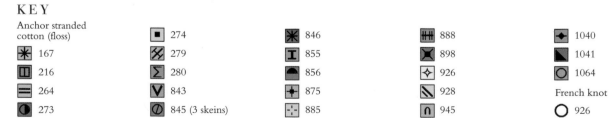

✳ 167	◼ 274	✳ 846	▦ 888	◆ 1040
▥ 216	✖ 279	I 855	✕ 898	◣ 1041
☰ 264	Σ 280	◗ 856	✦ 926	◉ 1064
◗ 273	⊘ 845 (3 skeins)	✚ 875	◣ 928	French knot
	V 843	⦂ 885	∩ 945	◯ 926

CHART 4

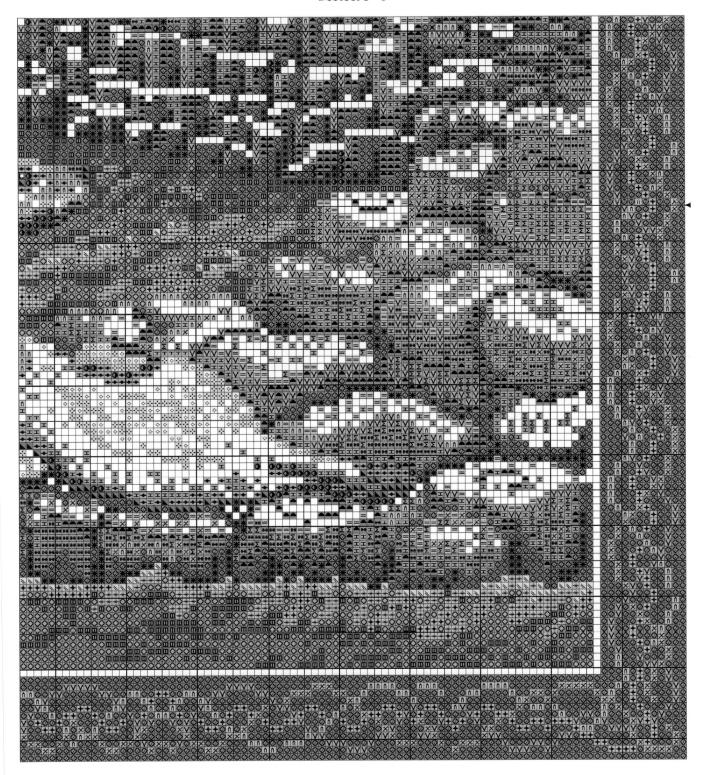

HIGHLAND STAG

DESIGN SIZE

12¾in x 10½in (32.5cm x 26.5cm) approximately

Stitch count: 179 x 146

MATERIALS

- 17in x 14½in (43cm x 37cm) 14-count Aida in beige (Coats No.0700)
- Size 24 or 26 tapestry needle
- Anchor stranded cottons (floss) as listed in the key

STITCHING GUIDELINES

The design is solidly stitched, apart from the unworked expanse of fabric between the picture and the beginning of the border, so it is simple to work from one side of the picture to the other or from the top to the bottom. I suggest working the actual picture before the border because if you want to change the size of the border or unworked

CHART 1

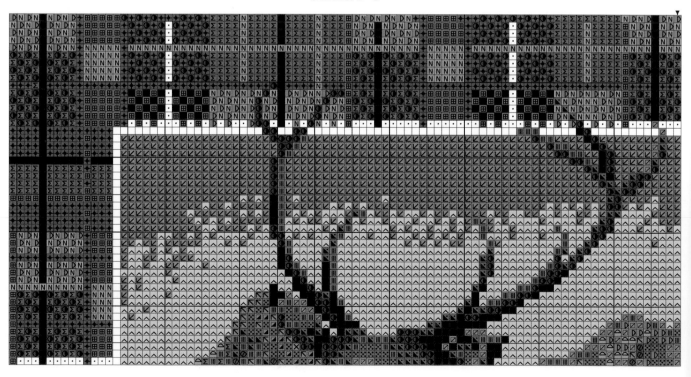

fabric, it is easier to see how this will look if the picture is already completely stitched. If you are intending to work from the centre of the design outwards, then prepare the fabric in the usual way

by marking the central horizontal and vertical lines (see Techniques, page 119).

All the stitches are whole cross stitches apart from the French knots on the stag's eyes. In order to make these visible without being too striking, use only one thread of Anchor 2 (off white) and wrap the thread twice around your needle before completing the stitch (see page 121). I suggest using a thread organiser to make working easier (see page 119).

Once the stitching is complete, remove the tacking (basting) or guidelines and then gently steam iron the design on the wrong side, being careful not to press too hard as this will flatten the stitches.

PLAN OF CHARTS

1	2
3	4

KEY

Anchor stranded cotton (floss)

▪	2	◨	246	◠	280	◑	380	Σ	1049 (2 skeins)
▲	160	◗	256	◥	281	◼	382		
◉	212	↑	265	◍	355	✚	1004	French knot
N	242	✕	266	◤	358	◪	1039 (2 skeins)	○	2
⊞	244 (2 skeins)	◸	267	▦	369	◩	1045		
		⊟	269	▥	374	D	1048		

CHART 2

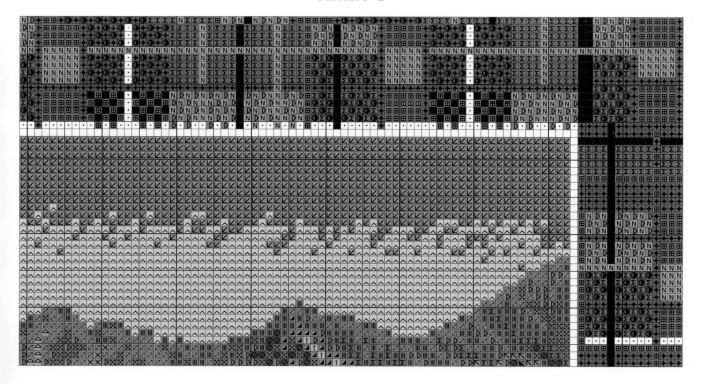

CHART 3

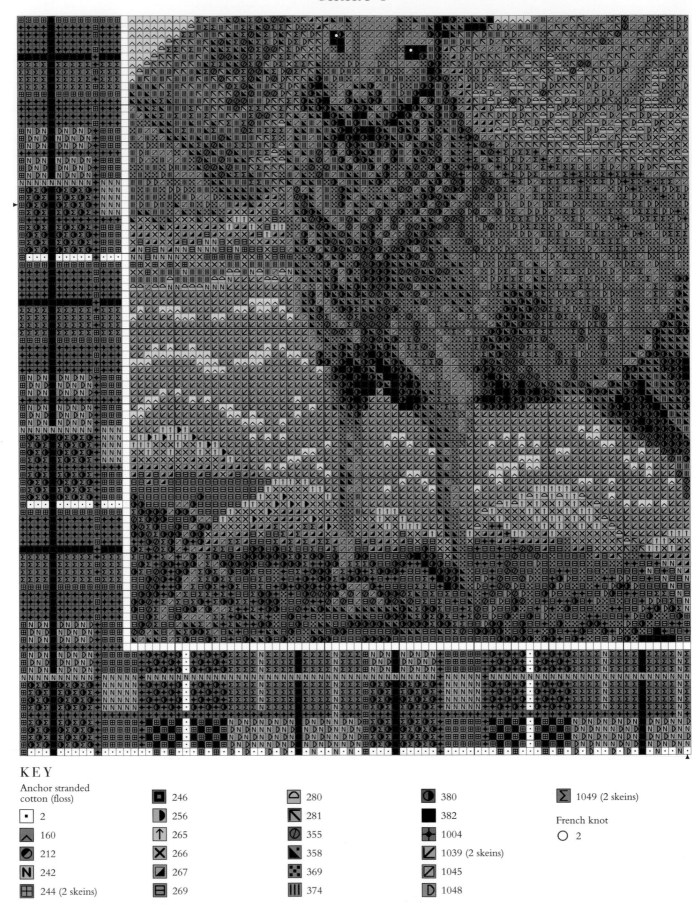

KEY

Anchor stranded
cotton (floss)

· 2	246	280	380	Σ 1049 (2 skeins)	
160	256	281	382	French knot	
212	↑ 265	355	1004	○ 2	
N 242	X 266	358	1039 (2 skeins)		
244 (2 skeins)	267	369	1045		
	269	374	D 1048		

CHART 4

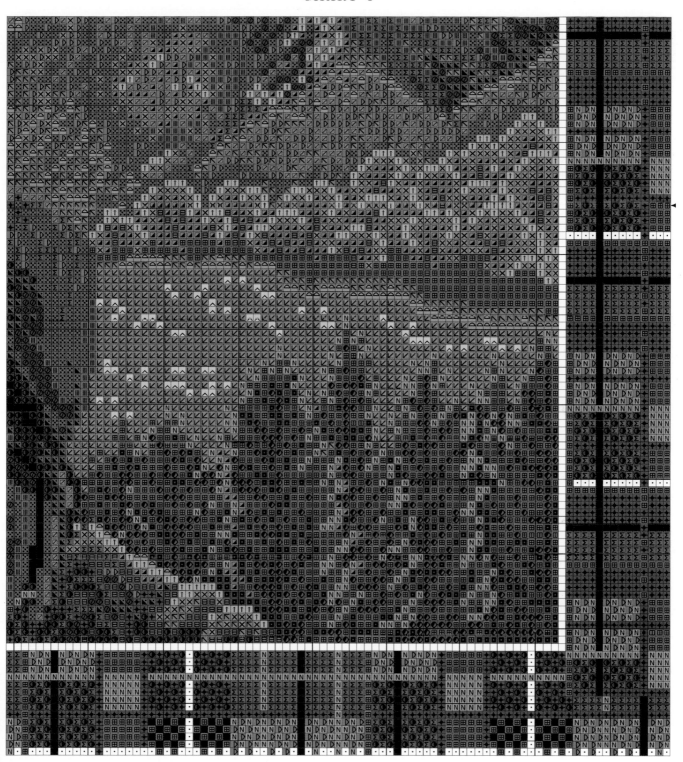

Next choose a picture frame and mount board to complement the design (see page 125 for framing advice). I find it very helpful to hold the mount board and frame next to the embroidery design to get the best idea of the end result. For this design I chose a pale sky blue mount board to balance the warm tones of the stag and the border. If you prefer to make the design up into a pillow, there are guidelines on making cushions in Making Up, page 123.

Tiger in the Lily Lake

I have had a mental image of a tiger

swimming in a lake for some time but held

back from actually making this design until

I saw a programme about tigers that made

me realise that most tigers actually *like* water.

I thought they were the same as my cats,

which avoid water like the plague. But when

I saw a tiger lying cooling off in a

shimmering lake with beautiful pinky-orange

water lilies all around him, I thought that I

could go ahead and stitch the scene.

RIGHT *This design is stitched on teal green fabric — which is fast becoming one of my favourite colours. The fabric itself becomes the greeny lake with pale blue catching the highlights of the rippling water.*

Ideally, I like to see all my subjects in the flesh and do little sketches and a watercolour or two, but at this point in my life I have to content myself with many different photos, and sketches done from memory from different television programmes. In this way I get as close as possible to realism which, hopefully, is decorative too.

The water lilies of course are an important element of the ornamental style of this design. Lilies love to grow in sunny lakes and spread rapidly, providing almost a carpet of colour in areas that remain undisturbed. They thrive in calm water and are not so dense where tigers swim and play amongst them.

Tigers are the largest of the 'big cats' and cannot bear immoderate heat, so at particularly hot times they bask in the shallows and cool themselves in lakes and rivers. They are also able to pursue their prey very easily in water as they swim extremely well and swiftly. They enjoy sunbathing and will often sleep on their backs in the milder heat of the late afternoon, enjoying the warmth – they have nothing to fear from other predators, only man and other tigers. They look deceptively cuddly but usually keep themselves to themselves. Unfortunately, due to extreme over

hunting in the past and now through loss of habitat, tigers are becoming increasingly rare and three of the original eight different subspecies of tiger are now feared extinct and the others are severely endangered.

I used many different colours to get the subtlety of the different shades of the tiger's coat. I have discovered, along with many other people, that although one thinks of a tree as having a brown bark and green leaves, this is very rarely true. The bark of a tree often has twenty different shades from pale green to purple-brown and the leaves are a glorious mixture of green, yellow, mustard and sometimes red – to name but a few. Using at least some of these colours tends to give a much more realistic image and that's what I really like to try to do when I am designing.

TIGER IN THE LILY LAKE

DESIGN SIZE
10¾in x 8in (27cm x 20cm) approximately
Stitch count: 153 x 107

MATERIALS
+ 15in x 11½in (38cm x 29cm) 14-count Aida in teal green (Zweigart No.626)
+ Size 24 or 26 tapestry needle
+ Anchor stranded cottons (floss) as listed in the key

STITCHING GUIDELINES
This design uses much of the teal green fabric to suggest the depths of the lake, so it is important to get the colour quoted above, or one very close in shade, or the end result will not look as illustrated here.

You will probably find it easier to start stitching from the tiger outwards, rather than counting through the lake. Either count in from the left side to the beginning of the tiger's head and work from

there or start at the centre point of the design (indicated by the arrows on the chart) and work from there. Remember to centre the design on the material so that there is an adequate surround for mounting the finished work (see Techniques, page 119). I suggest using a thread organiser to sort your colours and make working easier (see page 119).

All the stitches for this design are whole cross stitches using two threads of Anchor stranded cotton (floss), except for the tiger's whiskers. These are created with a couched long stitch (see Techniques, page 120). Work each whisker by making one long straight stitch from the tiger's face outwards, with two threads of Anchor 2 (off white), then catch it in two places on each whisker, a third of the way up and two-thirds of the way up, by bringing the needle up through a hole directly underneath the whisker, bringing the needle over

the top of the whisker and going back into the same hole. Pull the thread gently as you couch so that it is virtually invisible and gently darn in the thread on the reverse side of the work as you go. In this way, the tiger's whiskers look suitably whiskery and are kept neatly in place. If you are familiar with couching in embroidery, it is the same technique and very simple to do.

Once you have completed the stitching, remove the tacking (basting) or other fabric guidelines and gently steam iron the wrong side of the design. Be careful not to press too hard with the iron, otherwise the stitches become too flat and lose some dimensional aspect.

Mount and frame your embroidery (see Making Up, page 125). I chose a deep dusky-pink mount board to enhance the colours of the lilies, and finished the picture off with a moulded gold frame.

CHART 1

KEY

Anchor stranded
cotton (floss)

∷	2
III	208
ш	209
✕	210
I	225
F	244
∎	306
Ⅰ	307
∪	308
✕	309
Σ	355
↗	363
∎	382
∎	403
Ɛ	830
⅃	853
Z	877
╱	888
♥	1001
⌃	1021
✕	1022
V	1023
✳	1025
╱	1048
N	1062
▨	1064

Long stitch
—— 2

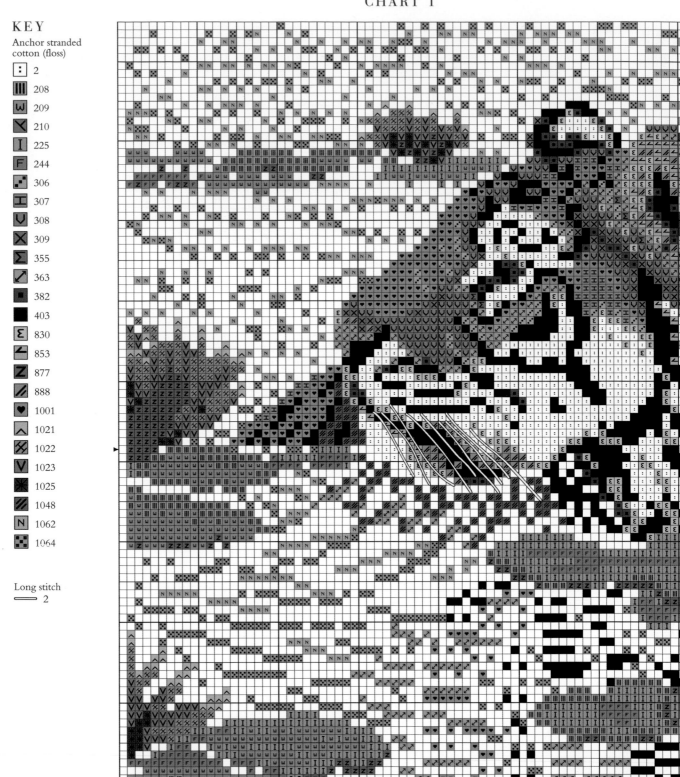

CHART 2

Tawny Owls
at Sunset

On most evenings, in the trees at the front

of my cottage, a pair of tawny owls call to

each other. The familiar long hooting

sound is the male and the sharp 'tu whit' at

the end is the female replying. I used to

think it was only one owl until I was

reading about owls and after that by

listening carefully, it was easy to tell that

there were, in fact, two.

RIGHT *These tawny owls were designed as
a picture but would be lovely as an inset for a cushion,
with a large border of rich brocade to bring it up to a
cushion size.*

It is such a pleasure to walk around the fields by the house, especially in the evening, listening to owls and other birds. There seems to be a special quality in the air at dusk; there is usually the sharp tang of wood smoke drifting across from different chimneys and looking at the sun setting and the first stars peeping out in the sky, I feel that at that particular moment, there is nothing more that one could possibly want.

I am fortunate enough to have large trees close by and a lot of open land in between, so I have wildlife literally on the doorstep and quite a variety of birds come to the bird table and to the hanging wire cages of nuts. (I have wire cages to stop the squirrels bolting down all the nuts as soon as they are put out – but they can still get some!) Once or twice, a sparrow hawk has paid a swift visit to the bird table but most birds of prey, like tawny owls, prefer to catch their own food. The tawny owl, like the well-known barn owl, likes wood mice and other small rodents to eat, which is rather helpful to us humans!

So, the tawny owls were a very immediate inspiration for this design, sitting in the horse chestnut tree close by. I know they are there because I can hear them but it is very difficult to catch a glimpse of them. Tawny owls are nocturnal unless they are very hungry and then they will sometimes hunt during the day, but because they are quite small birds, they are liable to be mobbed by other birds and even attacked by magpies if they are caught unawares in the day. They usually have a variety of regular song perches from which they hunt at night and they like to be really high up in the tree tops which makes it difficult to view them.

The scene I have stitched here is the view I sometimes manage to catch in the evenings with the sun going down in immense colourful glory, the light on the horse chestnut leaves making them glow as if they are on fire. Of course, we do not get sunsets like this all the time but they are truly spectacular when we do.

TAWNY OWLS AT SUNSET

DESIGN SIZE
8¾in x 9in (22.5cm x 23cm) approximately
Stitch count: 123 x 126

MATERIALS
- 13in x 13in (33cm x 33cm) 14-count Aida in mushroom brown (Zweigart No.781)
- Size 24 or 26 tapestry needle
- Anchor stranded cottons (floss) as listed in the key

STITCHING GUIDELINES

In this design it is important to get the right colour of Aida fabric, or something very close to that particular colour number, because the fabric which remains bare becomes a significant part of the owls. So, if you use a colour which does not suggest the body colour and feathers of the owls, it will not look like the finished design shown here. As the rest of the design is stitched leaving no bare fabric, it is easy to stitch it starting at the top left and working either from the top to bottom, or from left to right.

I tend to do both – following a particular colour downwards and across until that colour is stitched – but this is a matter of personal preference and enjoyment.

If you prefer to work from the centre point, then find and mark the centre of your fabric (see Techniques, page 119) and work outwards from that point starting with the colour given on the chart, which is Anchor 306 (topaz). Before you start stitching, I suggest sorting your threads on an organiser to make working easier (see page 119).

The stitches used in this design are all whole cross stitches using two threads of Anchor stranded cotton (floss), apart from the single French knots for each of the owls' eyes. These are worked using one thread of 926 (very light beige). These French knots need to be worked quite small so that the highlights of the owls' eyes do not protrude too much. I suggest wrapping the thread round the needle twice and making the tension firm before putting the needle back through (see Techniques, page 121).

Once the stitching is completed, remove the tacking (basting) or guidelines and gently steam iron the wrong side of the design, taking care not to press too hard and flatten the stitches.

The picture can now be finished off by choosing the colour mount board and frame that you like (see Making Up, page 125). I have used a teal green mount board and a gold frame, which works well with most colour schemes.

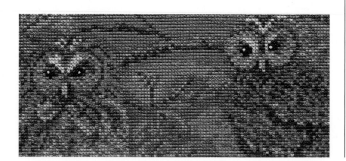

KEY

Anchor stranded cotton (floss)

Z	11
◑	13
N	209
Z	255
T	273
⟋	279
R	302
L	303
∎	306
X	308
✦	324
▦	326
●	382
■	683
⁒	830
▪	853
V	855
Σ	876
⊓	877
✳	878
◺	886
3	888
□	898
✧	926
S	945
⟌	1002
∩	1003
X	1004
▼	1041

French knots
○ 926

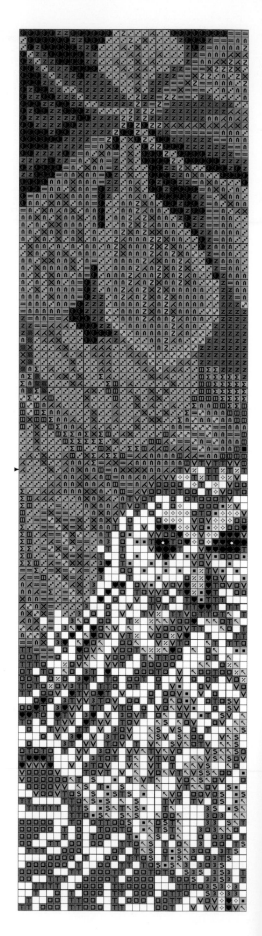

Wildlife Patterns

These two striking designs – Zebras at the

Watering Place and Giraffes in the Bush –

were inspired both by the beauty of these

animals and my fascination with their unique

coat markings. The studies feature the animals

in their natural African locations, each design

framed by the distinctive patterning of the

zebra and giraffe. The designs make

wonderful partners, either as cushions or

framed as pictures but they could equally well

act as focal points on their own.

RIGHT *The patterns of the giraffes' and zebras' markings stitched for these cushions, make a striking and decorative statement which would grace any light and airy space.*

Zebras at the Watering Place

I have always loved the amazing visual effect that a herd of zebras creates – they make a wonderful moving pattern in which you cannot see where one animal ends and the next begins. This clustering together is deliberate, to confuse their would-be attacker with the patterning of their stripes. It is also extraordinary that no zebras have exactly the same stripe pattern, just as no two people have the same fingerprint.

There were four species of zebra but the fourth species, the quagga, which only had the forefront of its body striped, has been hunted to extinction. The herds of the different species often graze in the same areas but do not interbreed. They remain separate but if they are threatened they all take flight together, the minority herd always running in the middle with the larger herd surrounding and protecting them, which seems such wonderfully instinctive behaviour.

The stripes of the zebra are obviously their predominant feature and over the years many theories have been put forward as to why zebras have stripes. One recent theory is that the stripes are actually a cooling system. Zebras have layers of fat, which insulate them from the enormous heat only under the black stripes and these black stripes get almost 10°C (50°F) hotter than the white stripes. This causes the hot, sweaty air to rise from these black stripes, making the air circulate, replacing the hot air with dryer, cooler air. So, in fact, it acts like a miniature fan.

Zebras, like other grassland species, need water and spend much of their non-grazing time in water, when there is plenty. They are a beautiful sight with their lovely silvery-white bodies *(continue on page 77)*

PLAN OF CHARTS

1	2	3
4	5	6

CHART 1

KEY

Anchor stranded
cotton (floss)

⚹	2 (4 skeins)
⋀	160
N	215
☉	216
↑	265
S	266
E	267
Ɛ	366
✕	367
Y	368
▦	382
■	403 (5 skeins)
V	843
⅄	845
⏃	851
T	855
Z	856
M	861
∩	874
▢	877
⋈	888
A	945
▪	1038
Σ	1040
H	1041

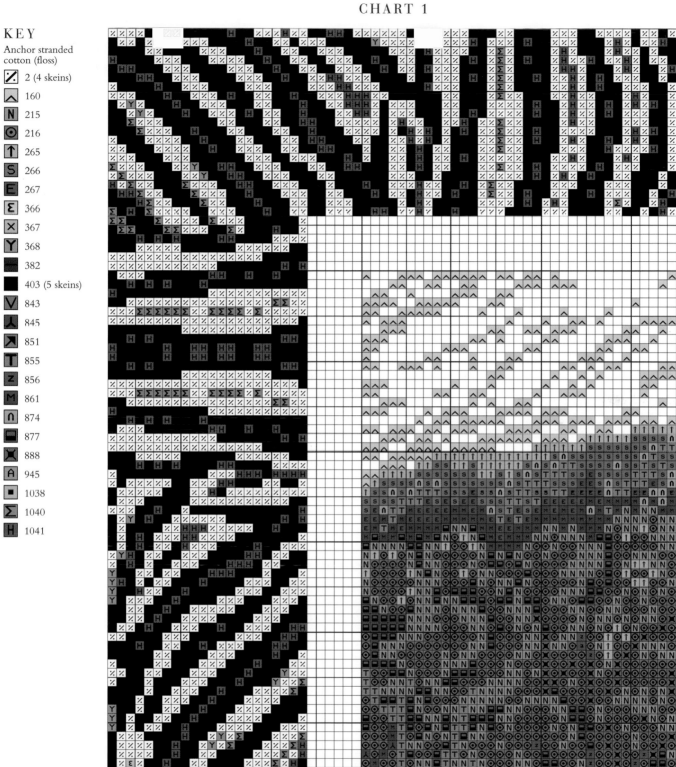

CHART 2

CHART 3

KEY

Anchor stranded cotton (floss)

Symbol	Color
✐	2 (4 skeins)
∧	160
N	215
⊙	216
↑	265
S	266
E	267
Ɛ	366
X	367
Y	368
▬	382
■	403 (5 skeins)
V	843
⅄	845
↗	851
T	855
Z	856
M	861
∩	874
▫	877
⊠	888
A	945
■	1038
Σ	1040
H	1041

CHART 4

KEY

Anchor stranded
cotton (floss)

Symbol	Number
⊿	2 (4 skeins)
∧	160
N	215
⊙	216
↑	265
S	266
E	267
Σ	366
X	367
Y	368
▨	382
■	403 (5 skeins)
V	843
⋏	845
⬈	851
T	855
Z	856
M	861
⋒	874
▭	877
⋈	888
A	945
▪	1038
Σ	1040
H	1041

CHART 5

CHART 6

KEY

Anchor stranded
cotton (floss)

◿	2 (4 skeins)
∧	160
N	215
⊙	216
↑	265
S	266
E	267
Ɛ	366
✕	367
Y	368
▬	382
■	403 (5 skeins)
V	843
⅄	845
↗	851
T	855
Z	856
M	861
∩	874
▢	877
✕	888
A	945
▪	1038
Σ	1040
H	1041

striped with brownish-black and the paler shadow markings between. It was a challenge when creating and stitching the design, to keep the zebras separate enough to be visible whilst still creating the patterned image that the animals themselves form.

Completing one design like this always gives me many more ideas for doing the same subject in different ways. I so enjoyed this design that I shall have to 'do' zebras again. One zebra on its own or many together – they are delightful creatures.

ZEBRAS AT THE WATERING PLACE

DESIGN SIZE
14¼in x 13⅞in (36cm x 35cm) approximately
Stitch count: 200 x 195

MATERIALS
- 18in x 18in (46cm x 46cm) 14-count Aida in Delft blue (Coats No.2529)
- Size 24 or 26 tapestry needle
- Anchor stranded cottons (floss) as listed in the key

STITCHING GUIDELINES
It is important to obtain the right colour of Aida fabric or one that is extremely close to that particular colour number, as the fabric is part of the water that the zebras are standing in and also part of the sky. If you do not use a similar colour, the end result will look quite different.

I have left a border of six unstitched holes around the zebras before beginning the border. If you would like to alter the size of the cushion for any reason, it is simple to do this by leaving more or less unstitched fabric, or by

working some more stitches of the border pattern.

The entire design is worked in whole cross stitches using two threads of Anchor stranded cotton (floss). Stitching will be quicker and easier if you arrange the thread colours on an organiser before you begin stitching (see Techniques, page 119).

I suggest starting at the centre of this design, finding and marking the centre of the fabric as described in Techniques, page 119. Work outwards from the central point, taking care not to rub the work already stitched. The stripes are enjoyable to work down, filling in the 'white' areas in between afterwards. Once the zebras are stitched, the picture starts to take shape.

When the stitching is finished, remove the tacking (basting) or guidelines and gently steam iron the fabric on the wrong side taking care not to press too hard and thereby flatten the stitches. To finish, chose a suitable backing fabric and make up into a cushion (see Making Up, page 123).

In this design, the blue material forms part of the lake and areas of the sky, which means that although it is quite a large design, there are less stitches than you think! To enhance the finished piece, I chose a closely patterned blue fabric for backing, which I also used for self-cording around the cushion.

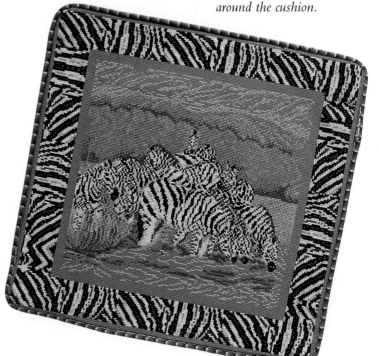

Giraffes in the Bush

Historically, mankind has always honoured giraffes, though at times this honour would seem somewhat cruel to us with our present day understanding of animals. For instance in 1826, a Masai giraffe was presented to Charles X of France by Muhammad Ali, the despotic Viceroy of Egypt. The giraffe, called Zarafa, was walked along the route of the North African slave trade enduring all manner of hardships and, after a quarantine period on the island of If, she was then walked up through France, astonishing the people who turned out en masse to marvel at her in each village and town that she passed through. She then made a triumphal entry into Paris in 1827, where thousands of people welcomed her after her 550 mile (885km) trek from Marseilles. This led in turn to a ludicrous fashion called 'a la Girafe', where Parisian ladies wore their hair coiffured so high that they had to sit on the floors of their carriages in order to travel anywhere. The men wore elongated ties and sporting hats in honour of the giraffe.

Giraffes, like zebras, each have a unique set of markings, with no two giraffes having the same pattern. Although the patterns on giraffes are not instantly as striking as that of zebras, the more one looks at their skin the more beautiful it seems. In fact their whole appearance is astonishing and when one sees them 'in the flesh', it is almost difficult to believe that they are real, so remarkable it is.

Their Latin name *Giraffa camelopardalis* literally translated means 'one who walks swiftly' (*giraffa*) and 'camel marked like a leopard' (*camelopardalis*). This was the name they were given when they were brought to Rome in about 46BC as they were deemed to be as big as a camel, with spots like a leopard!

(Continue on page 85)

PLAN OF CHARTS

1	2	3
4	5	6

CHART 1

KEY

Anchor stranded
cotton (floss)

Symbol	Number
S	215
◉	216 (2 skeins)
↑	265
U	266
T	267
Z	358 (3 skeins)
M	366
L	367
N	368
I	374
◢	375 (2 skeins)
⅄	381
▪	382
∕	387
‖	856
N	861
O	870
⊡	871
▤	877 (2 skeins)
Ɛ	885
F	888
‖	944 (3 skeins)
ш	945

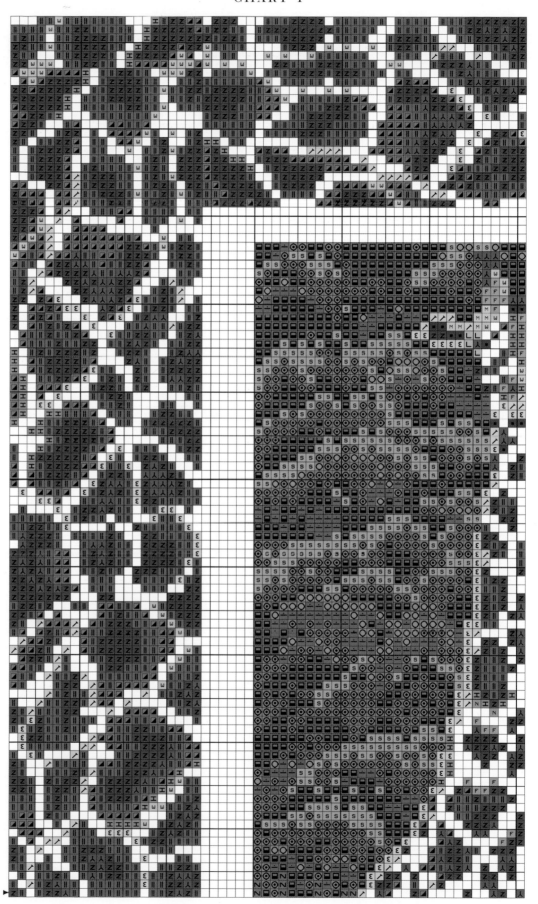

CHART 2

CHART 3

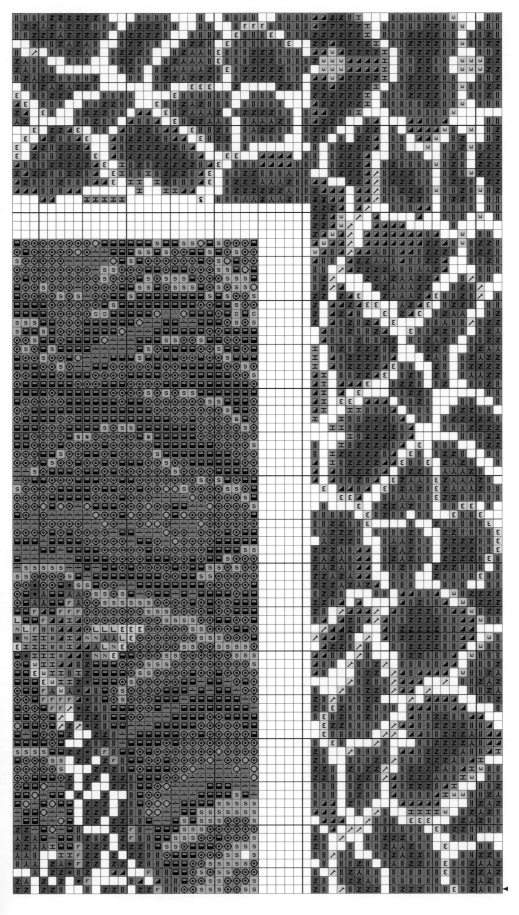

KEY

Anchor stranded
cotton (floss)

Symbol	Color
S	215
⊙	216 (2 skeins)
↑	265
∪	266
T	267
Z	358 (3 skeins)
M	366
L	367
N	368
エ	374
◢	375 (2 skeins)
⅄	381
▪	382
⁄	387
‖	856
Ν	861
O	870
⊟	871
▬	877 (2 skeins)
Ɛ	885
F	888
Ⅱ	944 (3 skeins)
ɯ	945

CHART 4

KEY

Anchor stranded
cotton (floss)

S	215
⊙	216 (2 skeins)
↑	265
U	266
T	267
Z	358 (3 skeins)
M	366
L	367
N	368
I	374
◢	375 (2 skeins)
人	381
▪	382
╱	387
‖	856
N	861
O	870
▬	871
▬	877 (2 skeins)
Ɛ	885
F	888
‖	944 (3 skeins)
W	945

CHART 5

Rabbits in the Vegetable Patch

Rabbits are rare visitors to my garden although

they are common in nearby fields where

I walk my dogs. The rabbits leap away only inches

from the dogs while they are busy following the

scent with their noses to the ground, too fixated

to look up and actually *see* the rabbits. When they

have finally followed the scent in circles to the

place where the rabbit has just hopped from, the

rabbit has long since disappeared!

RIGHT *I designed Rabbits in the Vegetable Patch as a runner
for a kitchen sideboard or small table but it would be lovely as a
picture too. To set the design off, I have framed it with fabrics.*

When the rabbit was introduced into England from France by the Normans some 900 years ago it was looked upon as a great asset – for food and for fur. I am afraid that it is now considered rather a pest. In those days, rabbits were to some extent farmed and were kept in a walled enclosure called a warren. This name has lasted and has come to mean any area where a number of rabbits live, so that we usually call a group of rabbit burrows, a warren. They even had a keeper, called a warrener, who fed them and protected them from any passing predators. The rabbits were let out into the fields to forage and then returned in the evening for shelter. Now, rabbits feed mostly at night and sleep most of the daylight hours.

The fact that rabbits escaped and increased hugely in number did not matter too much until agriculture became more intensive and the human population expanded too. Now rabbits are responsible for an expensive amount of crop damage and farmers try to keep their numbers down. They can also be a real nuisance in your vegetable patch if there are large numbers of them. The odd one or two, I think, are certainly tolerable guests. The rabbit's basic diet consists of the herbs and grasses found in hedgerows and the crops that farmers grow are eaten mainly because they are there, spread out in front of the rabbits like a feast.

I used a teal green fabric to work on for this design and the unstitched parts suggest the shadows between the vegetables and in the grass. It was a most enjoyable piece to design, choosing the soft fur colours of the rabbits and the bright colours of pumpkins, tomatoes, carrots and nasturtiums. The beautiful purple highlights of the artichokes against the green of their fleshy leaves makes a pleasant contrast.

PLAN OF CHARTS

1	2	3
4	5	6

KEY

Anchor stranded
cotton (floss)

✕	11	Σ	254	I	956
⊖	13	✗	255	⊞	1004
●	45	∧	298	◼	1015
⋀	92	⊔	303	⋁	1072
∑	100	←	324	⊙	1074
◩	203	▦	326	▭	1076
◆	204	◼	382	◣	1098
◥	206	⊠	855		
▪	209 (2 skeins)	◿	882		
Z	225 (2 skeins)	╱	888		
⊖	226 (3 skeins)	W	898		
◑	227	▼	904		
◿	241	⊓	905		
		S	945		

Long stitch
▬▬▬ 956

French knots
● 905
○ 956

CHART 1

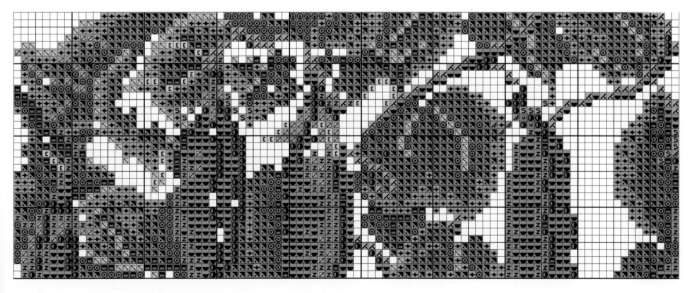

CHART 2

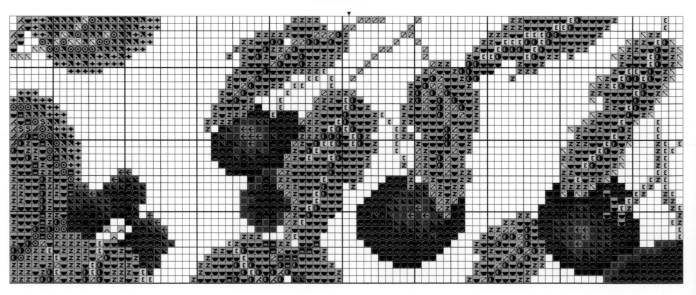

KEY

Anchor stranded
cotton (floss)

☒	11	Ɛ	254	I	956
◓	13	☒	255	⊞	1004
◕	45	⋀	298	◆	1015
⋀	92	L	303	U	1072
Σ	100	←	324	⊙	1074
◺	203	▦	326	▣	1076
◆	204	▣	382	◣	1098
◥	206	☒	855		
▪	209 (2 skeins)	◪	882		
Z	225 (2 skeins)	◪	888		
◓	226 (3 skeins)	W	898		
◖	227	▼	904		
◿	241	▮	905		
		S	945		

Long stitch
━━━ 956

French knots
● 905
◯ 956

CHART 3

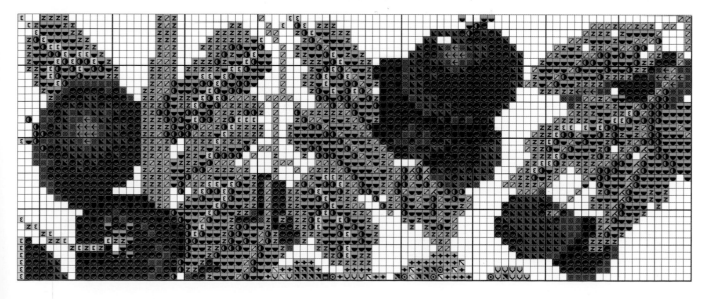

CHART 4

KEY

Anchor stranded
cotton (floss)

⊠ 11	◣ 206	⋀ 298	⊡ 898	⊙ 1074			
⬕ 13	◢ 209 (2 skeins)	⊔ 303	▼ 904	▣ 1076			
● 45	Ζ 225 (2 skeins)	← 324	⊓ 905	◪ 1098			
⋀ 92	◗ 226 (3 skeins)	▨ 326	S 945				
Σ 100	◑ 227	◪ 382	I 956	Long stitch			
◹ 203	◪ 241	⊠ 855	⊞ 1004	▬ 956			
◆ 204	Ɛ 254	◿ 882	▮ 1015				
	◺ 255	◿ 888	⋃ 1072	French knots			
				● 905			
				◎ 956			

CHART 5

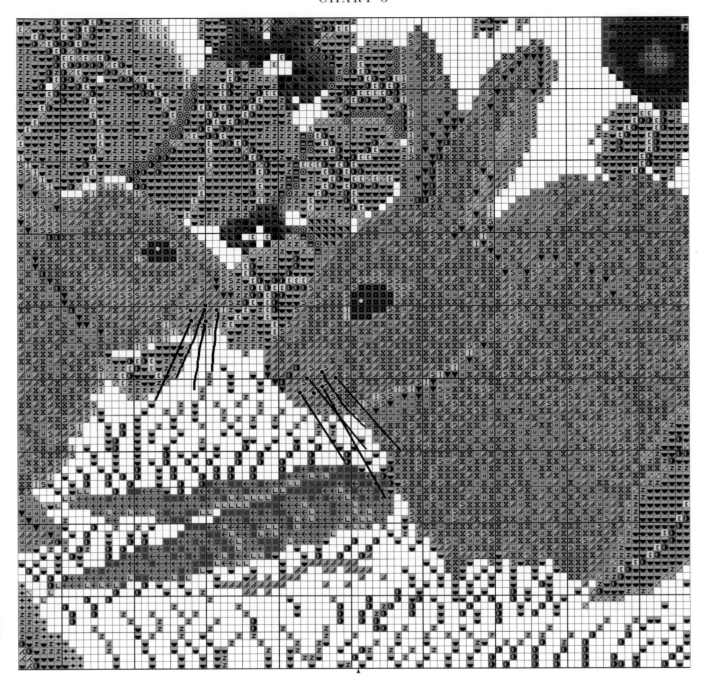

CHART 6

KEY

Anchor stranded
cotton (floss)

✖	11	◨	206	⌃	298	⊡	898	⊙	1074
◖	13	▪	209 (2 skeins)	⌐	303	▼	904	▣	1076
●	45	Z	225 (2 skeins)	←	324	▢	905	◣	1098
▲	92	◗	226 (3 skeins)	▦	326	S	945		
Σ	100	◐	227	▪	382	I	956		Long stitch
◥	203	◿	241	✖	855	⊞	1004	━━	956
◆	204	Σ	254	◿	882	◼	1015		French knots
		✕	255	◿	888	∪	1072	●	905
								◉	956

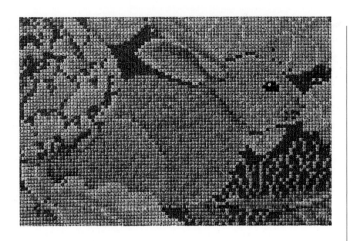

RABBITS IN THE VEGETABLE PATCH

DESIGN SIZE

19⅞in x 9in (50cm x 23cm) approximately

Stitch count: 278 x 128

MATERIALS

♦ 24in x 13in (61cm x 33cm) 14-count Aida in teal
green (Zweigart No.626)

♦ Size 24 or 26 tapestry needle

♦ Anchor stranded cottons (floss) as listed in the key

STITCHING GUIDELINES

This design uses the colour of the background fabric
to suggest the shadows between the vegetables and in
the grass and therefore it is important to use the
fabric colour given above or a colour that is
extremely close in shade, otherwise the completed
design will not look the same as the one shown here.

As this design is not solidly stitched, it may be
easier to begin stitching at the centre, so find and
mark the centre of the material (see Techniques, page
119). To make stitching quicker and easier I also
suggest you use a thread organiser (see page 119).

After doing this, find the centre on the chart
(indicated by the arrows on the sides) and start
stitching the nasturtium leaf where the central point is,

working outwards to stitch both of the rabbits. When
the rabbits are completed, you can work outwards from
either side until the rest of the design is finished.

This design is worked in whole cross stitches using
two threads of Anchor stranded cotton (floss) except
for the eyes and the whiskers. The eyes each have a
French knot worked in Anchor 956, light beige. Use
only one thread for this and keeping the tension
firm, wrap the thread twice round the needle before
putting it back through, as close to the point you
came up as possible (see page 121).

Each whisker (shown in black on the chart) has a
French knot in 905 at the base. Work the whiskers
themselves in couched long stitch (see Techniques,
page 120) using one thread of 956 (light beige). Start
by making one long straight stitch from the rabbit's
muzzle outwards. Catch the long stitch in two places
on each whisker, a third and then two-thirds of the
way up, by bringing the needle up through a hole
directly underneath the whisker, bringing the needle
over the top of the whisker and going back into the
same hole. Pull the thread gently as you couch so that
it is virtually invisible and darn in the thread on the
reverse side of the work as you go. This makes the
whiskers look long and whiskery but they are also
kept in place. If you are familiar with embroidery
stitches, this is the same technique that is used for
couching; it is very effective and simple to achieve.

Once the stitching is finished, remove the tacking
(basting) or guidelines and press the work on the
wrong side with a steam iron, taking care to press
gently so as not to flatten the stitches.

Make up the design as a runner and frame it with
fabric (see Making Up, page 125) or back it with a
suitable material so that it can lie as a decoration on
the top of a sideboard or chest of drawers.
Alternatively, frame it as a picture (see page 125).

Island Paradise

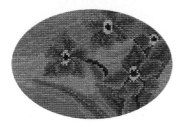

The island in this design is based on one of

the atolls in the Indian Ocean, where the

warm shallows consist of many types of

corals. These corals, with red algae, have the

necessary ingredients to form islands and

atolls – it is thought that the coral and algae

help each other to grow by transferring

nutrients between themselves thereby

reducing the loss of nutrients to the water.

RIGHT *This wall hanging is framed with material to add to the overall design (see page 122). It is enormous fun, finding complementary materials and once these have been fitted into place and machine stitched, it is exciting to give the imagination free rein and embroider into these fabrics.*

CHART 1

KEY

Anchor stranded
cotton (floss)

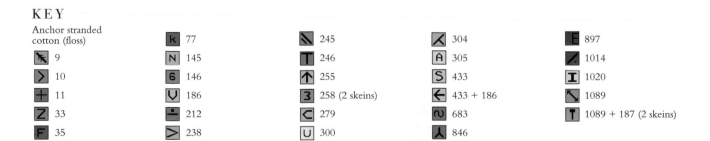

9	k 77	245	304	F 897	
10	N 145	T 246	A 305	1014	
11	6 146	255	S 433	I 1020	
Z 33	U 186	3 258 (2 skeins)	433 + 186	1089	
F 35	212	C 279	683	T 1089 + 187 (2 skeins)	
	238	U 300	846		

CHART 2

PLAN OF CHARTS

1	2
3	4

CHART 3

KEY

Anchor stranded
cotton (floss)

9	k 77	245	304	897
10	N 145	T 246	A 305	1014
11	6 146	255	S 433	I 1020
Z 33	U 186	3 258 (2 skeins)	433 + 186	1089
F 35	212	C 279	683	1089 + 187 (2 skeins)
	238	U 300	846	

CHART 4

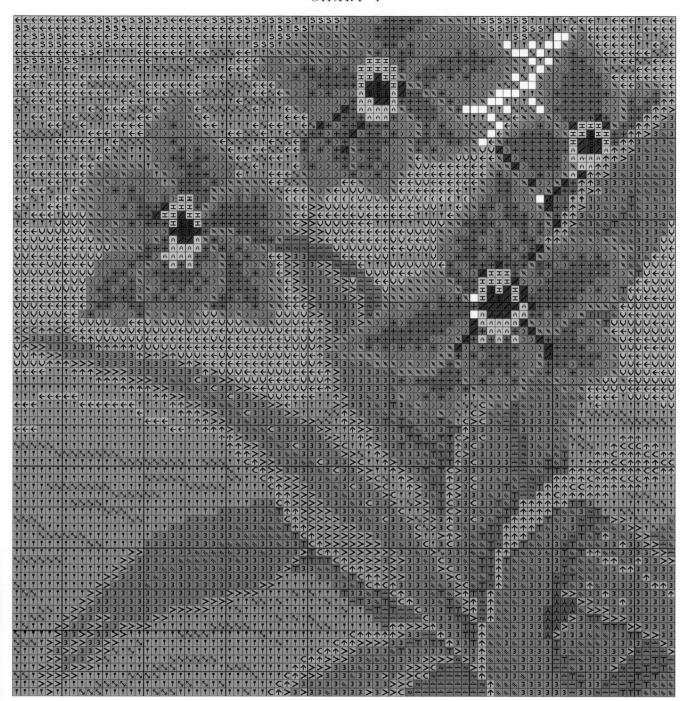

The Cactus Garden

The idea of a cactus garden did not occur to me until I saw some cactus paintings, which were so wonderful they inspired me to use them in a design. This was a perfect excuse for another visit to the botanical gardens at Kew in south London to sketch and photograph the cactus garden. There I found excellent examples of the golden barrel cactus and prickly pear, both of which I have used in this design, along with agaves and the giant saguaro.

RIGHT *This picture is an interesting and unusual subject and would be ideal in any room with its soft turquoise and yellow-amber colours. I chose a warm ochre mount board to make the whole effect of the cactus garden sunnier.*

Cacti and succulents provide an unparalleled diversity of shape, size, colour and texture. The soft, furry appearance of some is at complete variance with the reality of a tactile encounter with them, while others have easily visible spines of considerable length. Because of the great variety of cacti, it is possible to create a most interesting garden display, though we may not all have room for the giant saguaro which can grow as high as 50ft (15m) and live to be at least two hundred years old!

While looking at lizards to choose the right one for this design, I became fascinated by the variety amongst the different species. They are interesting creatures in a variety of colours, shapes and sizes and I find them a wonderful source of inspiration for many different kinds of designs. The lizard in this design is an American yellow-headed collared lizard. When another male threatens him, he jumps up and down, his feet entirely leaving the ground: other lizards do the reptilian equivalent of press-ups. Another interesting behavioural feature is the way they move. Most species use all four legs to move but some, including the collared lizard, do their fastest running on their two back legs so that they look like miniature dinosaurs moving at great speed.

Many of the behavioural characteristics of lizards are to protect them from predators. Their colours are often used as camouflage and many have tails which break off when touched. The piece of tail then wiggles to divert the predator's attention, allowing the lizard to escape. The tail regenerates but it is often shorter than the original, though still breakable. The chuckwalla lizard can retreat into a rock fissure and inflate its lungs so much that it cannot be pulled out. The horned lizard has the unattractive ability to spray blood from the corners of its eyes at any would-be attacker.

CHART 1

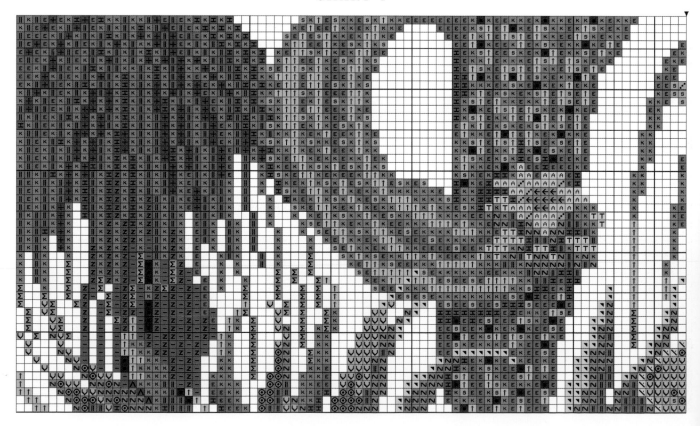

THE CACTUS GARDEN

DESIGN SIZE

11¾in x 9½in (30cm x 24cm) approximately

Stitch count: 166 x 134

MATERIALS

◆ 16in x 14in (40cm x 36cm) 14-count Aida in beige

(Coats No.0700)

◆ Size 24 or 26 tapestry needle

◆ Anchor stranded cottons (floss) as listed in the key

STITCHING GUIDELINES

The beige colour of the Aida fabric forms the background for the design so it is important to get the colour given above or one that is very close in shade, otherwise the end result will not look the same as the design shown here.

All the stitches in this design are worked in whole cross stitches using two threads of Anchor stranded embroidery cotton. For quicker and easier stitching, it will help to sort all your threads on a thread organiser (see Techniques, page 119).

KEY

Anchor stranded cotton (floss)

⊃ 167	E 268	↑ 324	✚ 381	S 945
☐ 168	I 269	3 326	■ 382	☐ 1001
Y 169	T 279	━ 355	∧ 851	Σ 1045
↑ 265	A 305	Z 358	◥ 875	◥ 1070
K 267	▪ 306	⁄⁄ 369	N 876	V 1072 (2 skeins)
	← 307	⁄ 374	‖ 877	⊙ 1074

CHART 2

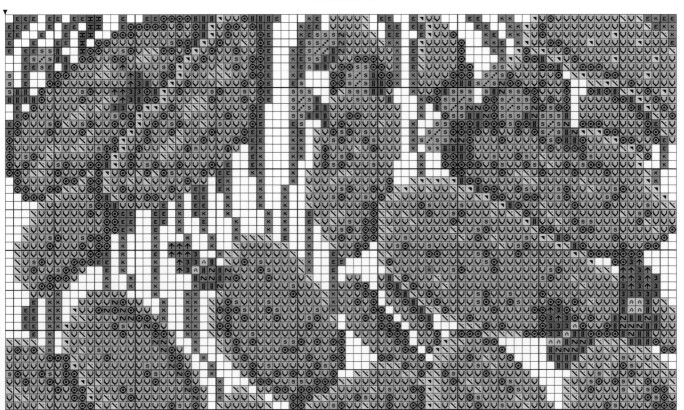

CHART 3

KEY

Anchor stranded
cotton (floss)

	E 268	↑ 324	✛ 381	S 945
⊃ 167	I 269	Ƹ 326	■ 382	⊡ 1001
⊡ 168	T 279	▬ 355	Λ 851	Σ 1045
Y 169	A 305	Z 358	◥ 875	◥ 1070
↑ 265	∙ 306	▨ 369	N 876	◡ 1072 (2 skeins)
K 267	← 307	◿ 374	‖ 877	◉ 1074

PLAN OF CHARTS

1	2
3	4

CHART 4

I suggest beginning this design at the centre of the chart and working outwards, so you will need to find and mark the centre of your fabric (see page 119). I chose to leave the lizard himself until last because I wanted to see how the cactus garden was looking before proceeding to stitch him, but this is a matter of personal preference.

When you have finished stitching, remove the tacking (basting) or guidelines and gently steam iron the reverse side, taking care not to press too hard and flatten the stitches.

Frame the project to complete it, choosing a frame and a mount board that suits the picture and the place in which you will hang it (see Making Up, page 125).

Rainbow Fish

This design came into being through a number of inspirations – some beautiful photographs of lily leaves viewed upwards through the water, a visit to the aquarium at Kew Gardens in south London and my own interest in tropical fish. When I saw these fish, which looked just like little rainbows flashing through the water, I really had to paint them and I thought immediately what a beautiful stitched design they would make.

RIGHT *I particularly wanted to stitch this design with embroidery threads to achieve the jewel-like, shiny, iridescent quality of the fish. I used Anchor Marlitt threads to do this as they have a good range of colours and the stitched effect is wonderful.*

normal living conditions.

Piranhas are among the better known species of characins and although they have a fearsome reputation, most are not only beautifully coloured but are also herbivorous and quite docile. We obviously hear much more about the carnivorous variety, the common red-bellied piranha, and they do go into quite a feeding frenzy if a bleeding animal (or person!) happens to be in the water close to them. Not a pleasant thought.

Human beings have been interested in fish keeping for many thousands of years. In Mesopotamia, the Sumerians kept fish in artificial ponds at least 4,500 years ago, and other early cultures that kept fish included the Egyptians, Assyrians, Chinese, Japanese and Romans. The

The fish I have chosen for this design and called rainbow fish are, in fact, cardinal tetras which are a small freshwater fish found mostly in the headwaters of the Amazon in South America. There are more than 1,400 species of characin, one of which is the tetras. They are often kept in aquariums by fish enthusiasts because of their brilliant colours and sociable behaviour. They are called a schooling fish, which means that they like to live in groups and form little communities; so in captivity they have to be kept in numbers of at least six otherwise they do not show their normal behaviour patterns and can even lose their colours if they are deprived of their

aquariums and artificial ponds served several purposes – they were decorative and entertaining and also provided a useful place for breeding fish to sell. The Chinese in particular developed the practice of breeding ornamental fish which were suitable for keeping in small containers. In fact, goldfish are a result of their endeavours and most of us are familiar with the beautiful oriental carp which feature so strongly in Chinese and Japanese art.

Up until recently, fish have not figured so much in western art but I hope you will enjoy stitching these lovely rainbow fish and will be as pleased as I was with the result.

RAINBOW FISH

DESIGN SIZE

13⅞in x 15¼in (35.5cm x 39cm) approximately

Stitch count: 195 x 213

MATERIALS

◆ 20in x 22in (51cm x 56cm) 14-count Aida in bright navy (Coats No.5225) (This was sufficient for the firescreen I used with its 16in x 18in (40cm x 46cm) aperture, but check it fits yours)

◆ Size 24 or 26 tapestry needle

◆ Anchor stranded cottons (floss) and Anchor Marlitt thread as listed in the key

STITCHING GUIDELINES

As the blue colour of the Aida fabric is used for the darker colour of the water, it is important to get the right colour or something very close to it so that the end result of the finished design is the same as the finished piece shown. I chose this Coats navy Aida because it was so much livelier than other navy blues I looked at.

I suggest working this design from the centre outwards so first find and mark the centre of your fabric (see Techniques, page 119). The actual centre on the chart is an unstitched square which you could temporarily mark for convenience with a stitch in a bright colour not used in this design. I also suggest using a thread organiser (see page 119) which will make stitching easier and quicker. Anchor Marlitt and similar shiny threads can be springy to work with but if you run each thread through a clean, damp sponge prior to use, the thread is much easier to use.

My suggestion then is to work the fish which begins just above the centre point, using cross stitch and two strands of the Marlitt, then to count down

from that and work the middle fish, and then count down once more and work the bottom fish.

The fins on the fish are worked in short running stitches, or backstitches if you prefer, going in the direction indicated on the chart and using only one strand of Anchor Marlitt. The fins can also be worked by making one very long stitch and couching it into place (see Techniques, page 120). This is done by bringing the needle up on the wrong side of the work to a point one third of the way up the long stitch, catching it in place by coming up through one hole, taking the needle over the top of the laid thread and putting the needle back down through the same hole. Repeat this process twice more at regular intervals on each long stitch as you make it to create a long, delicate curved stitch.

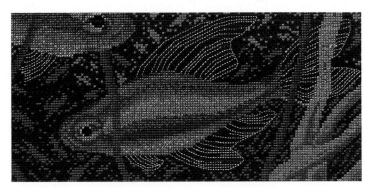

The rest of the design is worked in whole cross stitches using two threads of Anchor stranded embroidery cotton or two strands of Anchor Marlitt where indicated on the chart.

When the stitching is complete, remove the tacking (basting) or guidelines and gently steam press the wrong side of the work, taking care not to press too hard and flatten the stitches.

To make the design up into a firescreen see Making Up, page 124 or follow your firescreen supplier's instructions. This design would also make a delightful picture or could be used as the central panel in a big pillow or cushion.

CHART 1

KEY

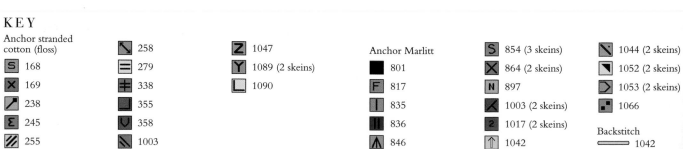

Anchor stranded cotton (floss)

S	168		
X	169		
/	238		
Σ	245		
⫽	255		

◢	258
≡	279
╪	338
◩	355
V	358
N	1003

Z	1047
Y	1089 (2 skeins)
L	1090

Anchor Marlitt

■	801
F	817
‖	835
‖	836
Λ	846

S	854 (3 skeins)
X	864 (2 skeins)
N	897
✕	1003 (2 skeins)
2	1017 (2 skeins)
↑	1042

N	1044 (2 skeins)
◣	1052 (2 skeins)
▷	1053 (2 skeins)
▪	1066

Backstitch

——	1042
——	1052 (2 skeir

CHART 2

PLAN OF CHARTS

1	2
3	4

CHART 3

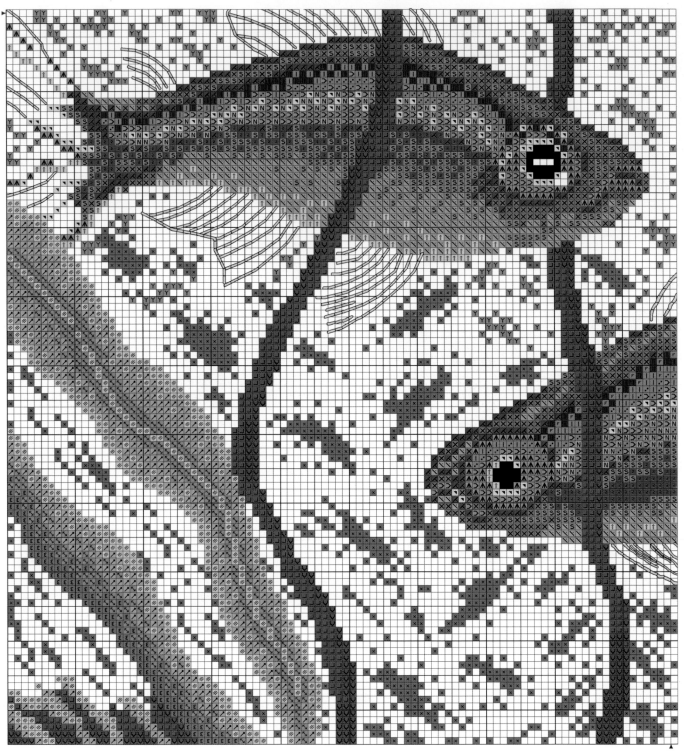

KEY

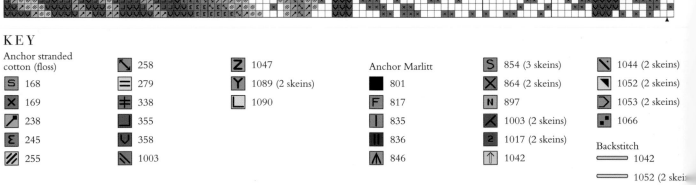

Anchor stranded cotton (floss)			Anchor Marlitt		
S 168	Z 1047		801	S 854 (3 skeins)	1044 (2 skeins)
X 169	Y 1089 (2 skeins)		F 817	X 864 (2 skeins)	1052 (2 skeins)
238	L 1090		I 835	N 897	1053 (2 skeins)
Ɛ 245	╪ 338		836	1003 (2 skeins)	1066
255	⊔ 358		846	2 1017 (2 skeins)	Backstitch
258	1003			↑ 1042	———— 1042
≡ 279					———— 1052 (2 skein
╪ 338	355				

CHART 4

Materials and Equipment

I have always kept my stitching apparatus to a minimum, which means for me, fabric, needle, scissors and threads (plus sketchpad and pencil for any design ideas.) This all fits neatly into a bag which I carry with me wherever I go so that any spare moments can be used stitching or drawing.

FABRIC

I have used a 14-count (14 holes per 1in/2.5cm) Aida fabric for all the designs in this book simply for ease of use and for the good colour range offered, although any of the designs can be stitched on evenweave, linen or a similar fabric. If you change the gauge of the material, that is the number of holes or threads per inch, then the size of the finished work will alter accordingly. If you change to an evenweave or linen fabric remember to work over two fabric threads instead of one block.

THREADS

I have chosen to use Anchor stranded embroidery cotton (floss), with some Anchor Marlitt and Kreinik thread for the projects as they offer an excellent range of colours and are generally tangle-free and easy to use. However, there is a thread conversion table on page 126 which gives equivalent DMC stranded cotton (floss) colour codes.

Two strands of stranded embroidery cotton (floss) have been used throughout, the exception being for the French knots, backstitches and long stitches. The skeins of stranded cotton (floss) consist of six strands and can easily be split into separate threads.

Anchor Marlitt can also be split and I have used two threads throughout for the cross stitches and one for backstitches and long stitches, although one strand of Anchor Marlitt consists of four threads not six.

The Kreinik thread I've used is one in an interesting range of metallic threads and I have used Very Fine Braids (#4) in places in the Peacock design. It is available from Coats Crafts UK (see Suppliers).

NEEDLES

I find it best to use tapestry needles for cross stitch as they have a rounded point and do not snag the material. They come in many different sizes and it is a matter of preference which size you use as long as the eye is big enough to accommodate the threads of embroidery cotton (floss) easily. I have suggested size 24 or 26 but if you find these too small, you could try a 22. Needles are nickel-plated or gold-plated – the latter being much smoother to work with.

NEEDLEWORK FRAMES

Whether you use a frame or not for your stitching is a matter of personal preference. I started stitching when I was working with Kaffe Fassett and frames were not in evidence at all. Speed was always of the essence and generally speaking, it is possible to work much faster without a frame. Personally, I find it less cumbersome and easier to work without a frame but the main thing is that you stitch in the way most enjoyable to you.

If you choose to work without a frame, be sure to watch your tension so that the work does not become distorted by uneven pulling of threads. If it does become distorted it can be restored to the proper dimensions by stretching afterwards.

Techniques

Cross stitch embroidery requires few complicated techniques but your stitching will look its best if you follow a few simple guidelines.

PREPARING THE FABRIC

Before commencing stitching, you should make sure that your fabric is at least 2in (5cm) larger all the way round than the finished size of the stitching, as this allows for making up. Check carefully the Design Size given at the beginning of each project and make sure that this tallies with the finished size that you require for your finished piece. For instance if you get a firescreen that is larger than the one shown in the book, then be sure to measure it and to buy sufficient fabric plus at least 2in (5cm) all the way round for mounting the finished piece.

Before beginning, it is a good idea to neaten the edges of the fabric either by hemming or zigzagging to stop the fabric fraying as you work.

MARKING THE CENTRE OF THE FABRIC

Regardless of which direction you are going to work the design from it is important to find the centre point of the fabric in order to place the work centrally on the fabric. To find the centre, fold the fabric in half horizontally and then vertically, then tack (baste) along the folds. The centre point is where the two lines of tacking (basting) meet. Alternatively, you could use tailor's chalk to mark the lines. This point on the fabric corresponds to the centre point marked on the chart. These tacked (basted) or chalk-marked lines should be removed on completion of the work.

USING A THREAD ORGANISER

It is a good idea to sort your thread colours carefully in good natural daylight and put them on a sorter card or organiser. You could use one of the commercially available organisers or make your own by using a hole punch to cut holes down the sides of a long piece of stiff card. Each shade to be used is then threaded through a hole with the appropriate chart symbol and colour number next to each thread. This will also make it easier to work by spotlight or daylight bulb in the evenings.

USING THE CHARTS

The charts in this book are extremely clear to work from as they include symbols as well as colour blocks, making it easy to discriminate between close shades. Each square on the chart represents one stitch. Each complete chart has arrows at the sides to help you find the centre point easily. In most cases the charts have been split over several pages, with the key repeated on each double page. You may find it useful to photocopy the charts and tape the parts together. Numbering every tenth grid line (the darker lines) is also a good idea as it will make counting easier.

STARTING AND FINISHING STITCHING

Avoid using knots when starting and finishing as this will make your work lumpy. Instead, leave a 'tail' of about 1¼in (3cm) at the back of your work and secure it by working the first few stitches over it.

To finish off the thread, pass the needle through some nearby stitches on the wrong side of the work, first in one direction and then in the opposite direction and then cut the thread.

WORKING THE STITCHES

All the designs are stitched principally with whole cross stitches. The other stitches used are backstitch, French knots and a couched long stitch. It is a useful practice to work in such a way that you are not rubbing the stitches already completed.

Backstitch

Backstitch is used to outline areas of cross stitch and to add definition. To make a backstitch follow Fig 1, bringing the needle up at 1 (or at the beginning of where the stitch is to lie), and down at 2 (or at the end of where you wish this stitch to be). Then bring the needle up again at 3 (or at the beginning of where you would like the second stitch to be). Keep repeating these steps as necessary.

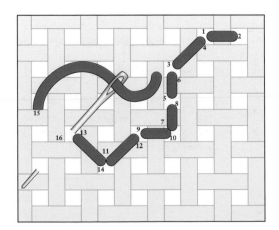

Fig 1 Backstitch

Couched Long Stitch

Couching is a technique whereby a thread is laid along the desired line in a design and is then held in place with little stitches. I have used this stitch for the whiskers in the Tiger in the Lily Lake design and Rabbits in the Vegetable Patch. You could also use it for the fins on the Rainbow Fish. The same thread can be used to make the long stitch and the subsequent little stitches or you could use a different thread to make the small stitches.

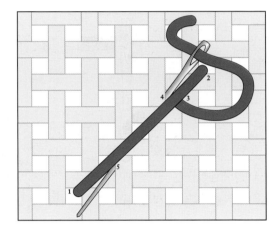

Fig 2 Couched long stitch

Start by bringing the thread through at the beginning of where you want the long stitch to be (number 1 on Fig 2), then push the needle and thread down through at the end of where the stitch is going to lie (2). Run the needle and thread up the work on the wrong side, catching it in neatly through the backs of other stitches to a point one third of the way up the long stitch, and bring the needle up through a fabric hole to the right side (3). Catch the long stitch by bringing the needle and thread over the top of the long stitch and putting the needle back through to the wrong side in the same hole, or as close to where it last came up as possible (4). Repeat this twice (or more) along the length of the long stitch.

Cross Stitch

A cross stitch has two parts and can be worked in one of two ways. A complete stitch can be worked singly (see Fig 3a) or a number of half stitches can be sewn in a line and completed on the return journey (see Fig 3b). Cross stitch worked on Aida fabric is usually worked over one block. If you decide to use an evenweave or linen instead, then you will need to work the cross stitches over two fabric threads in order for the stitches to be the same size.

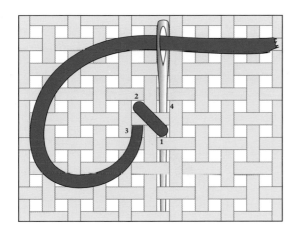

Fig 3a Cross stitch worked singly

To make a single cross stitch over one block of Aida, bring the needle up through the fabric at the bottom right-hand side of the stitch (number 1 on Fig 3) and cross diagonally to the top left-hand corner (2). Push the needle through the hole there and bring it up through the bottom left-hand corner (3), crossing the fabric diagonally to the top right-hand corner to finish the stitch (4). To work the next stitch, push the needle up through the bottom left-hand corner of the first stitch and repeat the steps above.

To work a line of cross stitches, stitch the first part of the stitch as above and repeat along the row until the end. Complete the crosses on the way back. Note: always finish the cross stitch with the top stitches lying in the same diagonal direction.

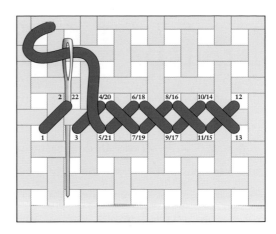

Fig 3b Cross stitch worked in rows

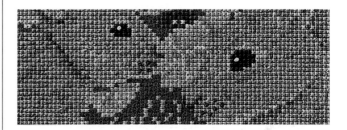

French Knot

French knots have been used as eye highlights in some designs (see detail above). To work, follow Fig 4, bringing the needle and thread up through the fabric at the exact place where the knot is to be positioned (1). Wrap the thread twice around the needle, holding the thread firmly close to the needle, then twist the needle back through the fabric as close as possible to where it first emerged (2). Finally, holding the knot down, pull the thread through to the back, leaving the knot on the surface, securing it with one small stitch on the back.

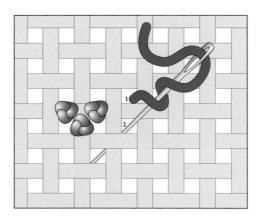

Fig 4 French knots

Making Up

There are countless ways to display cross stitch embroidery and you will no doubt have your own favourites. Below, I describe the main ways that the projects in this book have been made up.

WASHING AND IRONING EMBROIDERY

If it becomes necessary to wash your stitching, first make sure it is colourfast, then wash with a gentle cleanser (e.g. Woolite) in tepid water. Squeeze gently but don't rub or wring. Rinse in plenty of cold or tepid water and allow to dry naturally.

To iron your work, use a medium to hot setting on a steam iron and cover the ironing board with a thick layer of towelling. Place your stitching on this, right side down and press the fabric gently to avoid flattening the stitches.

The Rabbits in the Vegetable Patch design (above) is enhanced by being framed with complementary fabrics, while cushions (right) look attractive edged with piping.

FRAMING A DESIGN WITH FABRIC

Many designs are beautifully enhanced by being framed with complementary fabrics. Choose these fabrics carefully and decide how deep you would like the fabric borders to be. It is useful to take the embroidery with you when choosing fabrics so that you can hold the colours against the design.

Measure the length of each side of the embroidery and add on at each end the depth of the border plus a seam allowance. Cut the four strips needed, centre them and machine stitch them to the embroidery, stitching as close to the work as possible and making sure that the machine stitching of each side meets at the corners of the embroidery exactly. When you have done this, fold the work in half diagonally with the wrong sides together. You can then mitre the corners by stitching a line from the corner of the embroidery to the corner of the border panels. Do this on each corner and then trim the excess. Follow the same instructions for each fabric border that you wish to put on.

MAKING UP CUSHIONS AND PILLOWS

To make your stitching up into a cushion or pillow, choose a backing fabric which complements the stitching or, if you are going to frame the stitching with fabric, be sure that it tones with that material too. This is even more important if you are going to use the backing material for making your own piping. You will also need a cushion pad of the correct size.

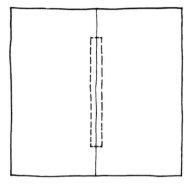

Fig 1 Backing a cushion

Cut the backing fabric using the finished work (plus the fabric frame if you are using one) as a guide, adding a further seam allowance of $^5/_8$in (1.5cm) all the way round. (If you are using piping or cording, see below right.) If you are going to use a zip fastener, cut the backing fabric piece in two, adding an extra seam allowance on each half for the zip (see Fig 1). Insert the zip in the centre back by stitching the top and the bottom and tacking (basting) the remainder. Insert the zip in the tacked (basted) part of the seam and machine it in. Then, with the right sides together, pin the backing to the embroidery. Machine stitch this as close as

possible to the stitching, or to the appropriate edges of the material framing the stitching. Machine all four edges if you have inserted a zip as above. Otherwise machine three sides and part of the fourth. After you have inserted the cushion pad, you can then slip stitch the part of the fourth side not already stitched.

ADDING PIPING

Edging a cushion or pillow with piping cord gives a good finishing touch. To make piping cord with the same fabric as the backing, simply buy sufficient cord and cut bias strips of fabric wide enough to cover the cord with a seam allowance of ½in (1.25cm). You may have to join the strips of fabric together to make the required length (see Fig 2). To do this, press the seams of the join open before covering the cord. Fold the

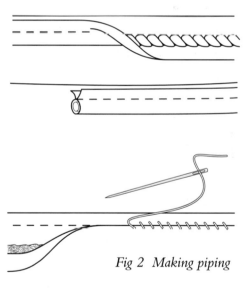

Fig 2 Making piping

strips around the piping cord and tack (baste) into place close to the cord. Then pin the piping to the right side of the embroidery so that the raw edges of the piping and the material are together. Pin and tack (baste) the backing fabric to the stitching (or the material framing it) by putting the right sides together, sandwiching the piping between and machine as above. Clip the corners diagonally and turn the right way out.

The Rainbow Fish design, beautifully mounted into an elegant firescreen (see Suppliers).

MAKING UP INTO A FIRESCREEN

There are many picture framers now who are willing to mount embroideries into firescreens but if you wish to do it yourself then you will need some thin plywood or hardboard, slightly smaller than the aperture of the firescreen. Centre your embroidery on the hardboard and check that it fits the aperture properly and is straight. Place the embroidery face down on some clean material and fasten it in place by lacing the back, stapling or taping it. Place the embroidery into the firescreen and put the backing board on. Most firescreens are supplied with a filler board and a backing board.

MAKING UP INTO A FOOTSTOOL

There are many upholsterers to whom you can take your finished work but if you prefer to do it yourself please read on. Most footstools are supplied with a dome-shaped piece of foam around which you can lace your finished work.

Start by carefully laying your finished work face down on some clean material or paper, then put the dome centrally on top of your stitching and draw around the perimeter of the dome with some tailor's chalk. Remove the dome, draw another line 2in (5cm) outside the first line and then cut out to the second line.

When you have trimmed your fabric loosely, tack (baste) two lines of stitching ½in (1.25cm) and ¾in (2cm) in from the edge. Leave a 6in (15cm) tail of thread at the beginning and end of the tacking (basting) on both lines so that you can use these to pull on and to draw the material in. Find the centre of the embroidery on the right side and gently pin it to the centre of the dome. Smooth the embroidery gently from the middle out towards the sides and pin in a few places. Then put the dome down on some clean material or paper and using the drawn threads, gather the fabric in on the underside of the dome. When you are satisfied that it is smooth and tight enough, tack (baste) or staple the material to the underside of the dome. It is then ready to place into the footstool and admire!

LEFT *The gorgeous Peacock design (see page 18) is stitched and mounted into a circular footstool.*

MAKING UP INTO A PICTURE

You could take your finished work to a picture framer and choose the mount board and frame you like or you can do the whole thing yourself. If you choose to do the latter, then you will need a box for cutting mitred edges on frames, some panel pins, a suitable saw, some hardboard (or thick card) and mount board. When choosing mount board, it is helpful to hold the edges of the mount board next to your finished work, with the frame at the outer edge to get the best idea of what the end result will be.

Mount your embroidery onto some thin hardboard or card and fasten in place by lacing it around the card or by stapling it. Decide on the frame size you require and carefully cut your frame pieces to the correct size, then panel pin them together. Using a mount cutter (which is by far the easiest) or a craft or Stanley knife, cut your mount board to the required depth. Place the mount board into the frame, then the embroidery. Finally, cut hardboard to size for the backing and wedge in with metal clips.

When framing an embroidery, the careful choice of mount and frame can set off a design beautifully.

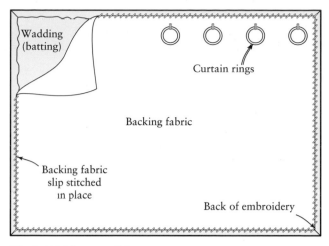

Fig 3 Making a wall hanging

MAKING UP A WALL HANGING OR RUNNER

A wall hanging is a lovely way to display embroidery, while a runner is perfect for adorning a table-top, chest of drawers or sideboard. If you wish to frame the stitched work with fabric borders, follow the instructions on page 122.

Wall hangings or runners can be backed with a suitable fabric which is best attached by slip stitching on to the embroidery (see Fig 3). Personally, I think it is much more fun to frame them with fabric and even to embroider into the designs on the fabric. If using interfacing or wadding (batting), as I have done with the Island Paradise wall hanging, then attach this by tacking (basting) it onto the wrong side of the stitching and fabric frames. The backing is then placed on the stitching, right sides together. Machine all three sides and part of the fourth and then turn right way out and slip stitch the remaining part of the fourth side.

To hang the wall hanging, attach curtain rings at regular intervals at a depth of 1½in–2in (4cm–5cm) from the top of the hanging on the wrong side. If you prefer you can make stitched loops. Slide a curtain rod or length of wooden dowling through these to suspend it from the wall, from cup hooks or other suitable fastenings.

Thread Conversion Chart

The designs in this book use Anchor stranded cottons (floss). If you wish to use DMC stranded cotton (floss), please use this conversion chart only as a guide, as exact colour comparisons between manufacturers cannot always be made, indeed some colours have no direct comparison. If you wish to use Madeira threads, telephone for their conversion chart on 01845 524880 or e-mail: acts@madeira.co.uk

Anchor	DMC	Anchor	DMC	Anchor	DMC	Anchor	DMC	Anchor	DMC	Anchor	DMC
1	B5200	175	794	265	471	366	739	877	502	1022	760
2	white	186	959	266	470	367	422	878	501	1023	3712
9	352	189	943	267	469	368	3828	882	754	1024	3328
10	351	203	954	268	937	369	729	885	613	1025	347
11	350	204	912	269	935	371	780	886	3046	1028	816
13	349	206	564	273	645	374	420	887	371	1037	3756
33	892	208	563	274	928	375	869	888	370	1038	519
35	891	209	910	277	830	380	898	889	610	1039	518
45	814	210	562	279	734	381	938	890	729	1040	647
49	3689	212	561	280	733	382	3371	891	676	1041	844
60	3688	215	320	281	581	387	ecru	897	221	1042	542
68	3687	216	367	289	307	388	3024	898	611	1043	369
69	3803	225	702	290	973	403	310	901	680	1044	319
77	3350	226	702	295	726	410	995	904	3787	1047	402
92	552	227	701	298	972	433	996	905	3021	1048	3776
98	553	236	413	300	745	683	500	926	613	1049	301
99	552	238	703	302	743	817	937	927	3755	1062	598
100	208	240	966	303	742	843	3053	944	869	1064	597
118	340	241	704	304	741	845	730	945	833	1066	3810
119	333	242	989	305	725	846	936	956	3047	1070	993
131	3807	244	987	306	3820	851	924	1001	976	1072	992
134	820	245	699	307	783	853	3013	1002	977	1074	3814
140	3755	246	986	308	781	854	370	1003	921	1076	991
142	798	253	472	309	780	855	3012	1004	920	1088	838
145	799	254	472	324	721	856	936	1013	356	1094	605
146	798	255	907	326	720	861	935	1014	355	1098	3801
160	827	256	704	338	351	870	3042	1015	3777	5975	3830
167	3766	257	905	340	919	871	3041	1016	3727		
168	807	258	904	358	433	874	833	1017	316		
169	806	261	3364	363	436	875	3813	1020	3713		
170	3765	264	3348	365	435	876	503	1021	761		

Suppliers

KIT SUPPLIER
Millennia Designs
Prospect Cottage, The Street,
Crookham Village,
Hampshire UK, GU13 0SH
Tel: 01252 616369
http://www.millennia.demon.co.uk
Most of the designs in the book will be available as cross stitch and needlepoint kits from Millennia Designs. Please write or telephone for brochure and information or visit the website. Millennia Designs also supply general needlework materials and ship worldwide.

THREAD SUPPLIER
Coats Crafts UK
PO Box 22, Lingfield,
McMullen Road, Darlington
County Durham UK, DL1 1YQ
Tel: 01325 394242
Fax: 01325 368822
Suppliers of all the threads used in the book and many of the fabrics.

FABRIC SUPPLIERS
Coats Crafts UK (as above)

Willow Fabrics
95 Town Lane, Mobberley
Cheshire UK, WA16 7HH
Tel: 0800 056 7811

FOOTSTOOL SUPPLIER
MacGregor Designs
PO Box 129,
Burton upon Trent
Staffordshire UK, DE14 3XH
Tel/Fax: 01283 702117

FRAME SUPPLIER
Shire Frames
Unit 100, Bunting Road
Northampton UK, NN2 6EE
Tel: 01640 718090
Fax: 01604 717941
At most of the big shows, phone for list of venues.

FIRESCREEN SUPPLIER
The Frame Workshop (Castle Crafts)
62 Broad Street, Hanley
Stoke-on-Trent
Staffordshire UK, ST1 4EU
Tel: 01782 286730
At most of the big shows, phone for list of venues.

ACKNOWLEDGEMENTS

My sincerest thanks go to Sally Jefferson at Coats Crafts UK for her enthusiasm, help and support for my work. This resulted in Coats supplying all the embroidery threads for the book and many of the fabrics and also supplying some of the stitchers, and I am extremely thankful to them for all of their help. A special thanks to Michaela Learner, one of Coats' stitchers, who must have eight hands to stitch so quickly and who does such beautiful work.

Warmest thanks go to my friends Janet and Chris Granger of Janet Granger Designs, who encouraged and helped me to work in more efficient and hopefully more interesting ways.

Special thanks to my friend and colleague, Sue Asher for her help with stitching and other aspects of the book.

Thanks also to Cheryl Brown at David & Charles for her encouragement and input in producing this book.

It was wonderful to have Michelle Garrett doing the photography for this book and grateful thanks to her for producing such beautiful and exciting shots.

Many thanks also to Shire Frames for the picture frames, the Frame Workshop for the Firescreen, Willow Fabrics for supplying Aida fabric and to MacGregor Designs for the wonderful footstool.

Finally, a heartfelt thank you goes to my children for being fairly patient when constantly hearing 'Not now, I've got a book to finish' *ad nauseam*!

Index